G Spot

for the

C Suite

Why Great Business Is Like Great Sex–
and How You Can Have More of Both

TRACY CALL

Cover Design: onegraphica.com

ISBN: 978-1-956955-65-1 (ebook)

ISBN: 978-1-956955-66-8 (paperback)

ISBN: 978-1-956955-67-5 (hardcover)

Contents

To Pam.

You're the reason I get out of bed every morning,
and the reason I can't wait to get back there at night.

Foreword

You can't talk about Tracy Call without discussing the Tracy Hug. It's a life-changing experience. Tracy gives you the exact amount of affection you need—always more than you think—and holds onto you until you feel safe, nourished and infinitely loved. It's the adult version of being swaddled as a baby.

As a friend and colleague of Tracy's, I've experienced several transformative Tracy Hugs over the years. But I was most moved by one she gave to my girlfriend, Sydney, during a trip to Mexico. Sydney's mother had died just four days prior, and as Sydney wept in Tracy's arms, I realized that it was the first time she'd truly grieved over her profound loss. Did the Riviera Maya's turquoise waters and rustling palm trees give her the emotional freedom to cry? No, it was Tracy's magical powers of intuition and compassion.

Those powers were, in fact, the reason we were in Mexico in the first place. Tracy had hired me to conduct "Walking the Love Path," one of my most popular workshops, for her and a partner. But here's the twist: She didn't want a Love Path for her and her romantic partner. She wanted to strengthen an important *business* relationship.

Tracy was elevating a woman to partner status at her multi-million-dollar ad agency, Media Bridge, and she wanted to do it right. None of my clients had ever applied a Love Path exercise to a professional situation. But then again, no one sees the parallels between personal and business relationships quite like Tracy.

Most people view starting a business partnership as an antiseptic process involving lawyers and paperwork. Tracy is different. She sees everything through the lens of relationships. Whether it's a sexual or business partnership, she knows that honesty, vulnerability, caring and trust apply. She also knows the stakes. If you want to feel joyful and complete, and if you don't want to self-destruct, then your connections need to run deep in all facets of your life. If negative patterns exist in one part of your life, then they'll probably infect other areas as well.

I had experienced this phenomenon myself. Growing up in Australia, I channeled a lack of parental love into a game of chasing achievements. I earned degrees in math, physics, finance, leadership, teaching and psychology. I graduated from one of the world's most elite military colleges, and I spent seven years in the Australian Defence Force.

Looking back, it's fitting that I also met my (now former) wife at an awards ceremony. We were both "go-getters." We started several businesses together. And we sold them for millions of dollars. But the root problems in our enmeshed personal and professional lives eventually collapsed upon themselves, leaving me lost, alone and needing to start over. That wouldn't have happened if I had read this book. I wish it had existed.

Today, I'm an executive coach, author, speaker and event facilitator who's been dubbed "The Business Mystic" for my ability to drive people to deeper levels of meaning and inspiration. But in Tracy, I've found a leader who inspires me. I've worked with thousands of people around the world, and no one "gets it" quite like her. She's hyper-perceptive, caring, inclusive, abundant and giving like few human beings on the planet. It's no accident that she's also an incredibly successful entrepreneur.

Tracy's superpower is her commitment to strengthening connections. I see it with her son, her wife, her employees, her clients. I saw it most clearly that day in Mexico. After giving Sydney a healing hug and a literal shoulder to cry on, she bought her a treatment and a massage. She didn't worry about how Sydney's grief might affect the Love Path she was paying for in a Caribbean paradise. She worried about Sydney. And we'll always be grateful for that gift of kindness.

I'm even more grateful that Tracy is now sharing her insights with a wider audience. Most of you will be transformed by these pages. Some of you might find them challenging—not only because Tracy is refreshingly blunt on matters of sex, but because she tears down so many long-held beliefs about personal and professional relationships.

Whatever your preconceived notions based on the provocative title of this book, I guarantee that it will inspire you to inventory your relationships. You might suddenly see negative patterns both at home and at work, and you might be shocked at how much those patterns mirror each other. These pages will make you think, reflect and definitely laugh. And after you turn the last page, you'll hopefully begin the process of forging healthier, happier and more fulfilling connections with the people you love.

Many of us spend years trying to escape. It's a fool's errand. Happiness starts with being present and intentional, awakening into the now alive with the certainty that this is the only place to be. Tracy gets this more than anyone I know, and that spirit radiates from her insights like rays of Mexican sunshine.

FOREWORD

In this book, Tracy tells it like it is. She doesn't pull any punches. She's both funny and profound. And she leaves you with a smile on your face, warmth in your heart and a flame in your soul.

Enjoy the journey!

—Finnian Kelly

Advance Praise for
G Spot for the C Suite

In nine sexy, sassy chapters, Tracy Call explains how women's capacity for empathy can help us read the room, connect with career-changing clients and take our networking game to new heights—while having mind-bending sex in our off-hours. "G Spot for the C Suite" should be required reading in every B-school in the country.

—Antonia Murphy, feminist entrepreneur
and author of *Dirty Chick*

"G Spot for the C Suite" is a bold and thought-provoking book that dares to examine the connection between understanding and enjoying our sexual identities and becoming professionally successful. Call presents a unique and compelling case for how embracing our sexual desires can lead to greater confidence and creativity in and out of the workplace. A must-read for anyone seeking to unlock their full personal and professional potential.

—Stephanie Dillon, multi-medium artist, philanthropist
and writer for *Rolling Stone* and *Artful Living*

ADVANCE PRAISE FOR G SPOT FOR THE C SUITE

The way Tracy writes will make you laugh and think while pushing you toward confidence and freedom in your work—and the best sex of your life. If you are a woman who has ever made herself smaller in a meeting, faked an orgasm or had a hard time being brutally honest with your needs and desires, "G Spot for the C Suite" is for you.

—Sarah Edwards, Founder and CEO of Haus of Sonder, Co-Founder of Fashion Week MN, fashion designer and influencer

Full of razor-sharp wit, spicy secrets and stimulating questions designed to push readers out of their comfort zone, "G Spot for the C Suite" is a vulnerable and provocative guide to intentional relationships and better performance from the boardroom to the bedroom.

Sue Hawkes, keynote speaker, Expert EOS Implementer™ and bestselling author of Chasing Perfection

Introduction

"Let's talk about sex, baby
Let's tell it how it is and how it could be
How it was and of course how it should be!"

—Salt-N-Pepa

Tina is a longtime friend and one of the most interesting people I know. She's brilliant, funny and attractive. She has every quality you'd want in a friend or partner. But I've never seen her truly happy.

One night after we shared a few glasses of wine, she started to open up about her marriage. Her partner didn't seem to notice or care about her anymore. The spark was gone, the sex nonexistent. She felt unattractive, invisible, past her prime.

Then I asked about her job. Her shoulders stayed slumped. Despite having worked at the highest levels in her profession, she felt increasingly irrelevant, devalued and stuck.

I recognized part of Tina's situation as the familiar weight of expectations that all professional women feel, especially entrepreneurs. Most women who run one business actually run two, because they also run the household. They grow their business and raise their family at the same time.

Expectations are different for men, especially at home. Being a woman requires extra commitment, extra patience, extra grit and extra care. You have to work twice as hard in both areas of your life to be considered a "success." And if you spend too much time in one realm, you feel guilty about the other. That's why I consider female CEOs to be the world's baddest badasses.

But something else hit me after listening to Tina, and I couldn't help but share it with her in the moment: her personal and professional relationships had always suffered from the same problems. You could literally swap the adjectives: "trapped," "irrelevant," "ignored," "under-appreciated," "washed-up," "invisible."

I realized that for as long as I've known Tina, she's felt stuck in the wrong career and married to the wrong person. She downplays her own assets until others stop seeing them as well. She's a perfectionist, so she's often overprepared, unspontaneous and afraid to do the wrong thing. Terrified of rejection, she ultimately settles for less than what she deserves. Less money. Less recognition. Less intimacy. Less sex.

"Oh my God, I have to write a book about this!" I blurted out. (Seriously, the idea for the book you're reading came to me in that exact moment.)

"A book about me? No thanks!" Tina said.

"No, a book about business and sex. Personal and business relationships. Don't you see how it's all the same thing, especially for women?"

Tina smiled. We know each other well enough that she wasn't offended.

"I'll call it *G Spot for the C Suite!*"

Tina almost spit out her Malbec with laughter. It was the happiest I'd seen her in years. We finished our drinks and talked about other things. But for days afterward, I couldn't stop thinking about our conversation, and the people I knew—mostly women—whose business and personal relationship problems mirrored one another.

I thought about the friend who took a job in education because her parents worked in that field, then married the guy her parents expected her to marry. She was miserable in both her personal life and her career.

I remembered my friend who left her wife and quit her job as a police officer at the same time.

I realized that a friend who claims to be wild and spontaneous in the sack is also a fast-and-furious entrepreneur.

I solved the puzzle of why a friend of mine has always been such a loner: when it comes to business partners and sexual partners, she avoids accountability.

I suddenly saw the parallels between a male colleague's behaviors in sex and business: he's a serial entrepreneur who's also in an open marriage. He has a core company while constantly starting new ones on the side, and he has a primary lover with others on the side as well.

And I thought about my business-owner friend who ended her sexual affairs and dissolved a toxic business partnership at the same time. After a hellish transition, she's thriving because she's recommitting to both.

I also looked at my own patterns. For me, everything clicked when I decided to ignore the myth that "Thou Shalt Treat Business and Personal Relationships as Complete Opposites." Those relationships definitely aren't identical, and I would never recommend sleeping with your clients or coworkers (that's a line I'll never cross). But I also think it's naïve to ignore how much sex and business relationships are psychologically intertwined. Just look at how we talk about our jobs:

"Cheryl is my work wife."

"I want people to fall in love with our brand."

"How can we penetrate the West Coast market?"

"Brian really put his dick on the table there."

"I think the client is cheating on us with another agency."

"Kyle definitely has big-dick energy."

We all bring consistent behaviors to our relationships. In both work and sex, I operate from gut instinct. I'm not scripted or rehearsed. I don't force myself or others to conform to unachievable ideals. I make decisions based on being in the moment, sensing each situation and reading (and pleasing) each person individually.

And it works. On the business side, I've grown my advertising agency, Media Bridge, into a $100 million enterprise that has earned a place on the Inc. 5000 list of fastest-growing private companies eight times since 2015. On the personal side, my wife, Pam, and I have been happily married for nine years, and former sexual partners often tell me that I top their "best sex I've ever had" list. These personal and professional successes don't involve the same people, and they may not seem to be related. But they are.

I've had my share of luck along the way, but I've also worked hard to push my relationships to a higher level. Now I want to help the Tinas out there do the same. Maybe you're one of them: unhappy, dissatisfied, even traumatized by the state of your personal and professional relationships. You need fresh eyes. Someone to help you discover the root causes of your issues. To assure you that it's okay. It's all part of the journey. And life can get better if you truly want it to.

I'm your woman.

My goal with this book is simple: by telling my story, I want to give you that extra jolt of confidence, that little push to make a positive change and feel more joy in your relationships. We all crave those screaming orgasms that give us the best high on the planet (if you don't, then you've never had one). So why demand anything less orgasmic from your professional life?

Your sex life and overall relationship with *intimacy* can teach you more about business than anything you'll find in an MBA program. While men can certainly benefit from the insights I share here, women will feel them more deeply. Our challenges in the bedroom and the boardroom are unique, and many of us row against the current to achieve agency in both.

My commitment to you is this: when you're done with this book, you will …

- See the parallels in what causes your personal and professional relationships to thrive or suffer.

- Recognize the areas in your life where passion desperately needs to make a comeback.

- Feel the courage to eliminate guilt and shame as limiting factors in your relationships.

- Know when "doing the work" will (or won't) solve the problem.

- Find the G spot in all areas of your life, and help others find theirs as well.

I feel like we're about to get between the sheets. Are you ready? Are you open? Are you excited? Then sit back, relax and let me take the lead. This is gonna feel good ...

—Tracy

Before We Take Our Clothes Off ...

This book is about breaking boundaries, but let's set a few down first. I compare certain aspects of business and sex in the pages that follow, and I don't apologize for it. The parallels are too strong to ignore, and we need to talk frankly about them.

Business and sex both involve intimate relationships with other human beings. They both involve attraction, trust, vulnerability, commitment and consent. They're both ultimately about giving and receiving pleasure. And come to think of it, they can both involve exchanging money for services rendered.

But to be clear, I don't actually believe in mixing the two. I don't sleep with my clients or employees, and I'm in no way recommending that you do, either. So don't take my choice of words literally. Take my analogies for what they are: an attempt to make useful points in an entertaining way.

Okay, enough anticipation. Let's make out.

PART I: SEXPLORATION

Are you in touch with your identity and sexuality? Your passions and fetishes? Are you confident in who you are, what you have to offer and what gives you pleasure? Are you comfortable in your body and eager to get naked? Or are you scared and ashamed, pretending to be someone you're not and in need of a coming-out party?

Chapter 1:
What's Your "Orientation"?

*"Do we have to worry about who's gay and
who's straight? Can't we just love everybody
and judge them by the car they drive?"*

—Ellen DeGeneres

On a crisp fall Saturday afternoon in Anoka, Minnesota, my mom and dad raked leaves in our front yard as I stood under a birch tree and daydreamed. Moments of solitude were common when I was 8. But suddenly an idea popped into my head that I had to share with my parents.

I marched up to them and declared, "I want to marry a girl!"

The rakes stopped. My parents didn't expect to hear those six words from their adopted daughter and only child. They looked at me, at each other, then back at me.

"Okay, honey, that's fine," my mom said in her Minnesota way. The rakes went back to scratching leaves.

My parents pretended that nothing had happened in that moment, but I knew better. I felt liberated. As I headed back to my birch tree, I knew that in another, more mysterious and vague way, I would never hide my truth again.

Sexy Business Secret #1

To be good in both business and sex, you need to figure out who you are. If you constantly adapt to other people or try to be who you're supposed to be, then you'll never be happy.

"When did you know?"

I always felt different from other girls. I mean, why did my friends insist on brushing Barbie's hair when her boobs were obviously so much more interesting?

To be clear, I wasn't exactly repulsed by boys. Far from it. In fourth grade, I kissed Brian underwater at the local swimming pool. In sixth grade, I made out with Mike as his brother timed our kisses with a stopwatch. In seventh grade, Steven pulled out a condom and asked me to have sex with him. (I turned him down because my birth mother got pregnant with me when she was only 16. Also, I knew there was something missing between me and boys.)

If you didn't already know it, sexual orientations are a real thing, not a "lifestyle." They're also messy, sometimes complicated and often unpredictable. We're always discovering new things about ourselves, and our self-awareness moves on its own time schedule. This is also true about professional orientations, by which I don't necessarily mean your job. I mean that thing in life that you're truly passionate about and feel you were meant to do.

> "Most of us know our sexual orientation far earlier than our professional one, but that's not cut and dried, either; it's a spectrum."

We all have that friend who knew by age 5 that they wanted to be a doctor, teacher or actor. And that's exactly what they ended up doing. Their focus and drive might have been shaped by early experiences, but it was also innate. On the other hand, many people are still bouncing around in their 40s and 50s, trying to figure out what they want to be when they grow up.

Most of us know our sexual orientation far earlier than our professional one. But that's not cut and dried, either; it's a spectrum. I define my sexual orientation as lesbian not because I'm attracted exclusively to women, but because I feel a deeper emotional connection to women than to men. As I explored my sexuality growing up, I realized that men are a "nice place to visit, wouldn't want to live there" situation. Women are home.

My path to discovery was also affected by the cultural environment I grew up in. Acting on my attraction to girls was unacceptable and sometimes dangerous in the '80s and '90s.

We've come a long way since then, but let's not kid ourselves. Today, people like me live every day knowing that simply being who they are can put their lives at risk.

On the professional side, many people rub up against family expectations and taboos when it comes to making a living. Dad is a sales manager who scoffs at your love of painting. Mom expects you to get an "Mrs." degree instead of going to law school. I know a dozen people who have done exactly what their parents expected them to do both personally and professionally. None of them are happy.

Nature vs. Nurture

Being adopted gives me an additional perspective on sexuality and professional orientation. On the professional side, my adoptive parents are retired teachers. Education is in their blood, not media or pop culture. They couldn't care less about who makes the commercials they see on TV, let alone who buys the airtime for them, negotiates the prices and makes sure they run at the right times. I, on the other hand, have never felt the urge to teach in a classroom. I've been attracted to advertising and entertainment for as long as I can remember. Not just the ads themselves, but everything that goes into them.

On the sexual side, I've always felt more libido-driven than my parents. Their hand-holding strikes me as affectionate and adorable, but not carnal. My sensuality volume is cranked 80% higher. When I'm into someone, I want to do more than hold hands.

As an only child, I sometimes felt different in my family— that is, until I met my biological relatives. That experience made a potent argument for nature over nurture. On the sexual side, I once caught my biological grandparents making out in their hotel swimming pool when they visited me in college. (Some people might have been horrified by this. I smiled and thought, "My people!") On the professional side, I learned that a high percentage of my blood relatives work in media, advertising and entertainment. My people again.

Coming Out

Especially for women, having the courage to be yourself sexually is a lot like having the confidence to start your own business. When I talk about "professional orientation," I mean not only *what* you feel compelled to do for a living, but also *how* you feel compelled to do it. My sexual awakening started under that birch tree when I was 8, but my professional coming-out happened after I graduated from college.

I sold radio commercial airtime for a large media company in the Twin Cities, and I knew I was in the right industry. But I was also growing more disillusioned with each managerial change. It all came to a head when my manager called me into his office one day. Our conversation went something like this:

"You know that nightclub client of yours?"

"Yeah, they're great."

"Tell 'em we're raising their evening rates."

"Why would we do that?"

"We just are."

"But they're a loyal client. Why would we raise their rates for no reason?"

"Just do it, okay?"

The company in question was a St. Paul nightclub that had advertised on our stations for over two decades. They were a model client. They spent more money with us each year. They never canceled a spot (a big headache in the business), and they always paid cash in advance. I used to drive there on Friday mornings to pick up wads of bills to fund the next week of radio ads. I loved them, and I wanted to help them succeed.

My manager, on the other hand, felt no emotional connection to this business or the human beings who owned it. To him, they were just another revenue stream, another line on a chart that needed to go up and to the right each quarter to make him look good. By executive order, he was changing the nature of my relationship to this client from "caring" to "transactional," and that offended me on a deep level. I thrived on helping small-business owners and their employees. He wanted to hit his arbitrary revenue numbers, and he was making a classic power move.

Raising my client's media rates felt so wrong that it made me physically ill—like someone telling me that I have to have sex with a man. I gave my manager a two-word response to his command: "I quit." I couldn't live by someone else's bad values; I had to set my own. As with my sexuality, this wasn't a choice for me. It was an acknowledgment of a deeper truth: I don't like people telling me what to do when I know what's right.

This marked the beginning of my entrepreneurial awakening. If I wanted things to be done right, I had to do them my way. My professional orientation came into focus just as clearly as my sexual one. I was a lesbian who loved men but felt more emotionally connected to women. And I was a media entrepreneur who knew there was a better, more caring and ethical way to help businesses grow.

I was in my mid-20s, and I was ready to get busy.

Afterglow

Being happy and fulfilled in both the bedroom and the boardroom starts with knowing and accepting who you are. We all have sexual and professional orientations. Our drives can be fluid to some degree, but they always point us somewhere. To succeed, you have to know what you like and how you like it. Embrace it. Fight for it. Enjoy it.

5 Questions

1. Why are you in your current job and career?

2. Does your work feel meaningful to you? Why or why not?

3. Do you feel like you're doing what you were meant to do, or are you still wondering what you want to be when you grow up?

4. Is there another profession you've always thought about exploring but have been afraid to for some reason?

5. What do you most want to accomplish as a professional?

Chapter 2: The M Word

"Good sex is like good bridge.
If you don't have a good partner,
you'd better have a good hand."

—Mae West

Doing the five-finger shuffle. Badgering the witness. Paddling the pink canoe. Flicking the bean. Stuffing your envelope. Minding the gap. Finger painting. Visiting the safe deposit box. Jillin' off. Saucing the taco. Diddling Miss Daisy…

You know what I'm talking about. When it comes to sexual activities, the M word produces some of our most colorful euphemisms. Unfortunately, it also arouses more than its share of judgment. Funny, because almost everybody does it. One study found that 92% of men and 76% of women have masturbated, and most people do it regularly.[1]

That's a good thing. Because in both sex and business, sometimes you need to DIY before you DITO (Do It To Others). And especially for women, societal shaming about taking matters into your own hands—or at least one of them—can prevent growth and discovery in all facets of life.

So let's get over the squeamishness right away. Don't pretend you've never shucked the corn or auditioned the finger puppets. As the old saying goes, "95% of people masturbate. The other 5% are lying."

Sexy Business Secret #2

Figuring out what gets you off professionally is a lot like figuring out what gets you off sexually. It requires self-exploration. Women face unique challenges in this realm because so many people heap shame on female pleasure.

---

[1] Survey conducted by sex toy company Tenga and research firm PSB, drawing on data from 13,000 respondents ages 18 to 74 in 18 different countries. https://www.tenga.co/press/TENGA_2020_US_Report.pdf

Busting the M Myths

Masturbation is a basic human function, yet we're not allowed to talk about it. When it comes to your happiness as a professional, this rejection of "humanness" is self-destructive. Especially for women, it produces a warped sense of strength and weakness. Denial is "strength"; anything less than perfect is "weakness." As a result, you can never say "I don't know," "I screwed up" or "I'm sorry." You can never admit that in most ways, you're no different than anyone else.

Is there anything we've been fed more bullshit about than masturbation? Depending on your age and religious background, you may have heard at some point that low-fiving causes everything from blindness and infertility, to mental illness and health problems during your period.

In reality, masturbation is associated with tons of health benefits. According to medicalnewstoday.com, "[S]exual stimulation, including stimulation through masturbation, can reduce stress, release tension, enhance sleep quality, boost concentration, elevate mood, relieve menstrual cramps, alleviate pain, and improve sex."

> "If you could put masturbation's benefits into a pill, you could charge $2,000 a bottle for it."

One study even found that women who masturbate have happier marriages than those who don't. Sorry, guys, but you're not the only source of pleasure for the women in your life. Sometimes they need a little something to fill the gap, so to speak.

If you could concentrate masturbation's benefits into a pill, you could charge $2,000 a bottle for it. Yet the M word still gets a bad rap. When people drone on about nothing, we make the jerk-off gesture. When someone acts self-absorbed, we accuse them of "mental masturbation." Does the act of ménage à moi deserve this unfair treatment? Not at all. As an expert in both M words (marketing and masturbation), I think it's time to give masturbation the rebranding it deserves.

Practice Makes Perfect

The first person I had sex with was a guy we'll call Kyle. We were both in college and both virgins, so you'd probably assume that our experience was like those awkward "first times" portrayed in movies and on TV. It wasn't. In fact, it was amazing. Kyle's vigor delivered five orgasms, and if I hadn't told him I was done, he'd probably still be going at it.

Never one to be shy about sex, I asked Kyle how he accomplished such an amazing feat. He told me that he masturbated to improve his endurance. I didn't feel a strong emotional connection with Kyle, but I applauded his commitment. Malcolm Gladwell famously wrote that mastering any skill requires 10,000 hours of practice. Kyle proved this just as much as the Beatles did. Come to think of it, both Kyle and the Beatles caused a lot of women to scream with pleasure.

Masturbating makes sense because it's the best way to discover your own body. *Gee, this feels good. You know what would make it feel even better? If someone did it to me!* It's not hard to make an evolutionary case for masturbation as a kind of "sneak preview" that makes people want to have more sex and produce more babies, though I don't think Darwin had much to say on the subject. He was probably too busy masturbating.

Kyle was a skilled lover because he had the humility to admit he needed practice. He masturbated to learn about himself, and then he became great in bed. I've had my share of practice, too. I've masturbated since I was 2. I'm serious. Most people's first memories are of getting a puppy, falling out of their crib or getting sick. Mine is of the stuffed koala bear I used to hump in my bedroom. Hey, it offered a way better angle than my Santa Bear. It was also a lot more satisfying than straddling the metal bar I rode as a kid in the front of shopping carts.

Buttering the muffin has continued throughout my life. A few years ago, I got so bored on a fishing trip that I mentally masturbated and actually brought myself to orgasm. I felt like a new superhero in the Marvel Comics universe. *Now teaming up with Black Widow: Rosy Palm!*

Most people don't share my intense prowess for spelunking the she-cave (okay, I made that one up), but I'm not sure why we fail to see masturbation as the vital practice field that it is. Whether it's trying new moves or building greater stamina, training for the big O is like training for the big W-I-N. It's also an underrated means of seduction: seasoning the meatloaf in front of your partner can really get things going.

But even solo Hand Solo can be an effective practice tool. Putting it back into business terms, what's masturbation but a means of intelligence gathering, knowledge transfer and spreading "best practices"?

The M Word Meets the V Word

For women, the M word is closely related to the V word. Not that one, the other one: *vulnerability*.

If you're someone who pretends that you never masturbate, or who acts offended or grossed out by the mere mention of it, then as a professional, you're probably a perfectionist, or someone who has a hard time acknowledging mistakes or admitting what you don't know.

The women I know who fall into this category are high achievers. Some grew up in ultra-religious families. They might have even been taught that masturbation is a sin, and that any intimate touch outside of making babies is impure and should be repressed. As a result, they're ruled by shame. They build walls around themselves and see invulnerability as the ultimate virtue.

As these women mature and understand sex better, they come to a crossroads: some choose to rebel, free themselves from the shackles of impossible demands and double standards, and embrace their humanness. Others double-down on perfectionism and live lives ruled by judgment and repression. Both types can achieve success in business, but only one can experience happiness.

My advice to people who fall into the repressed category is simple: relax. It's okay. Everybody poops. Everybody fucks up. And everybody masturbates. Including you. You're human. Now give yourself a hand.

Hitting the Ceiling

As you can tell, I think highly of masturbation. But while it's an important tool for achieving orgasmic success, it generally won't give you the full pleasure you deserve. In other words, being a party of one has limits that you can only overcome by exploring your sexuality with someone else.

In this sense, the woman who limits herself *only* to masturbating is like the entrepreneur who hits a ceiling by trying to do every job by herself. Every entrepreneur starts off as a party of one. You're the CEO, head of sales, VP of operations and IT manager all rolled into one. But you can't stay that way forever.

In business and in sex, personal and professional growth eventually requires bringing in another person. Or more, if that's your thing. No judgment.

Afterglow

Masturbation is undeniably normal, healthy, human and, when you think about it, slightly ridiculous. To succeed in sex and business, you need to accept that *you're* normal, human and slightly ridiculous. For women, masturbation can help you get more comfortable with experimenting, failing, satisfying your own curiosity and asking others to bring you the same pleasure that you bring to them.

5 Questions

1. As a child, were you taught that masturbation is bad and something to avoid, that it's a normal human activity, or nothing at all?

2. Is it easy for you to admit mistakes and acknowledge things you don't know?

3. Are you a perfectionist in both your personal and professional lives?

4. Do you think of vulnerability as a strength or a weakness?

5. Have you ever tried something on yourself and then shared that experience with a sexual partner? Did it make you super-squeamish to even read that question? Why?

Curious?

The Joy of Sex has sold over 12 million copies and has been translated into over a dozen languages, but it's not a sexy book. That's because the #1 killer of good business and good sex is the insistence on following a rigid playbook. (Also, those '70s illustrations are just plain creepy.)

Life isn't about control; it's about being curious. There's no one-size-fits-all in business or sex. You can't say "for every branding project, the client must do this," or "every entrepreneurial business under $5 million in revenue must follow this exact media plan." You also can't say to your lover, "We need to do this act, at this time, in this way."

Most of our need for control comes from fear and anxiety. Much of that comes from shame. People raised with shame about their bodies tend to feel shame around sex. Carrying that shame into your professional life is a playbook for frustration and resentment.

Want to experience the joy of sex and the joy of business? Pay attention. Lose your fear of vulnerability and embarrassment. Throw away the playbook. And just be curious.

PART II: SEDUCTION & FOREPLAY

Let's talk about flirting, wooing, courting and crushing. Does landing a client feel a little like bedding a lover? Do you enjoy attracting talent almost as much as you love attracting sexual partners? Do you feel like the rock star you are in your personal and professional lives, or have you lost your mojo in both areas?

Chapter 3: Chemistry

"I always hoped for this spark of chemistry to let me know that this was the guy. But it never came. And by no small coincidence, neither did I."

—Molly Harper, *Nice Girls Don't Have Fangs*

"Don't kiss me back."

That's what he whispered in my ear as we started making out in the stairwell. I had just met him, and I didn't even know his name, but I already trusted him and was willing to do anything he asked. As his lips worked their magic, I gradually shifted into his rhythm until we became one person. He was teaching me more than a new way to kiss. He was showing me a whole new way to be sexual.

I'd gone to the Iowa State University athletic building for a quick run. I didn't expect to be distracted by an Adonis lifting weights on a bench. We started flirting the second we spotted each other. With each loop around the track, I took in a different part of him. His deep brown eyes and hair. His broad, wrestler-like upper body under his oversized tank top. His dancer's legs, slim but strong, with smooth thighs and defined hamstrings. When he smiled at me after the seventh lap, the sexy little gap between his front teeth pushed me over the edge.

I ran an extra mile around the track, slowly filling in a fantasy. By the time he put down his weights, I was drowning in sweat.

"Come here," he said, his voice confident but not cocky. I jogged toward him as if we were already lovers. Within minutes, we were going at it in the stairwell.

As soon as we started kissing, I knew something was different about Ian (yes, I eventually learned his name). His kisses were soft, tender and—there's just no other way to say it—sexy as hell. I had kissed lots of boys before that. Now I realized that they all had no idea what they were doing. Kissing Ian was like having your first glass of really good wine. Suddenly, everything else tastes like swill.

On our walk home, Ian and I shared the basics of our lives. He was from California. He was studying entomology. He was both a wrestler and a dancer. (I called it!) In fact, he was such a good dancer that he drove to Des Moines on the weekends to win contests and earn spending money.

We had immediate chemistry that led to marathon makeout sessions for months after that, but we always stopped short of sex. Ian wouldn't go all the way because he was a devout Mormon. I didn't tell him that I was a lesbian, partly because I wasn't ready to come out yet, and partly because … did I mention he was a devout Mormon?

Making out with Ian was different from anything I'd experienced to that point. I could do it all day long. Each time we kissed, the world melted around me. His touch was electric. His hands found the right places. My lips would be soft the entire next day. He always left me wanting more.

I didn't want to have sex with Ian, but I did want an education. So I would stop him mid-makeout to ask him about what he was doing.

"Tell me how you kiss like that."

"The key is to do it with the inside of your lip, because that's the softest part. Like this."

"Wow, that's nice. Show me again."

"Happy to."

"I think I'm getting it, but one more time would be greaaat."

"Okay."

"Yeah, just one more … "

Ian and I didn't last as a couple. We couldn't, given who we were. But our breakup accelerated when I discovered that he was sleeping with his ex-girlfriend (so much for devout Mormonism). Even though things ended badly—and even though we never had sex—the Ian Affair provided valuable lessons in chemistry that I've since applied to all of my relationships.

Sexy Business Secret #3

The chemistry you feel with a lover is different from the chemistry you feel with a client, colleague or coworker. But if you don't feel a spark in your current romantic relationship, then you probably don't feel one in your job, either.

What Is "Chemistry"?

Chemistry is mysterious by nature. You can't really explain why you feel attracted to one person and not another. That's what makes chemistry so compelling.

On a sexual level, it's mostly physical, of course. How many times have you heard a person say, "I knew as soon as I saw [him or her] that we were going to get married"? What drew my eyes to Ian as I ran around that track at Iowa State? Why did I want to drink in every part of him as I got close? Why did I feel so much trust in a person I'd just met?

Business chemistry lives more in the head than the loins. Maybe you're an idea person who's found that special someone who gets your vision and wants to make it happen. Maybe you've met someone who has the same sense of humor about your current job as you do. In my case, I feel instant chemistry with other entrepreneurs. Show me a scrappy person who started a business, is passionate about growing it and willing to live out of their car until they start making money, and I'm all in.

> "The jolt I get when I meet someone I want to work with is different from the flood of dopamine I've gotten when I meet someone I want to sleep with. But they're equally intense."

We've all felt a mysterious electricity around another person, personally and professionally. Maybe it happened when François, the exchange student from Paris, walked into your high school history class. Maybe it happened last weekend at a conference when you met Patty from Indianapolis and realized that you face similar challenges as female executives trying to navigate a "bro" company culture.

I've felt these two kinds of chemistry throughout my personal and professional lives. One is sexual; the other isn't. The jolt I get when I meet someone I want to work with is different from the flood of dopamine I've gotten when I meet someone I want to sleep with. But they're equally intense.

In business, I've felt the nonsexual brand of chemistry with colleagues, employees, clients, you name it. A few examples:

- On paper, Renters Warehouse founder Brenton Hayden and I are opposites who would have never crossed paths outside of work. But I felt instant chemistry when I met him in 2010. I won him over by showing him how I could double the value of his media buy. He won me over with his entrepreneurial grit (he really did live out of his car when he started his business). Our "30-minute meeting" lasted hours, and I stayed up all night developing his media plan. Today, Renters Warehouse is the nation's largest single-family property management company.

- As soon as real estate entrepreneur Kris Lindahl saw me walking toward his office for our first meeting, he prank-called me. "I'm at Media Bridge. Where are you?" After I apologized for the mix-up, he popped out from around the corner, laughing his ass off. I loved him immediately, and we would work together for the next several years to help make him a household name in his markets. Today, Kris Lindahl Real Estate is one of the largest team-owned real estate brokerages in the country.

- I felt business chemistry from the moment I sat down for lunch in the Minneapolis skyways with Sara Darling of It's Just Lunch. I knew she would be an incredible client. She's also been a great friend. Media Bridge has been her constant partner in building the country's largest It's Just Lunch franchise system, and I was honored to have her speak at my wedding.

"Chemistry" is a word that we throw around without ever defining it. That's because analyzing it is like learning how a magic trick is done: it ruins the magic. Here's one example of what you find when you research the nature of personal chemistry:

> "In a 2016 study in *Frontiers in Psychology*, researchers proposed that [chemistry] 'is a natural addiction that evolved from mammalian antecedents 4 million years ago as a survival mechanism to encourage hominin pair-bonding and reproduction.'"[2]

Sexy, eh?

Actually, chemistry with another person does involve actual chemistry. If you so much as think about a person you have chemistry with, your brain can react as if you're doing a line of

---

[2] https://www.ncbi.nlm.nih.gov/pmc/articles/PMC4861725/

cocaine. Sometimes it's even more powerful, and you feel an overwhelming desire to make the object of your crush a mixtape.

In my case, I get butterflies. I can't eat or sleep because I'm so excited. I think, *How can I push this relationship even further? How can we connect even more?* On the business side, something hijacks my brain after a great first meeting with a potential client. I don't think *Let's have sex!* I think *Let's build the greatest media plan in the history of advertising!* I feel it after big wins, like when Media Bridge won Agency of Record for the NCAA Men's Final Four in 2019 and the Women's Final Four in 2021. But I can also feel it when a client calls just to get my opinion on their campaign.

Bottom line: there's more than one way to get turned on, but only if you're receptive to it. Chemistry doesn't just happen. If you're open to feeling it with people in your personal life, then you're probably the same way in your professional life. Similarly, if you're shut down in one area, then you're probably shut down in the other.

I was open to meeting Ian, and we ended up making out in a stairwell. Similarly, I'm open to making connections with colleagues, mentors, clients and employees. Things don't always work out, and that's to be expected. But every encounter teaches me something new.

The idea for this book started when I realized that my friend Tina had lost all passion in her marriage and her career. The challenge started with her, because she wasn't fully open to feeling chemistry. Something about it scared her, yet her chemistry-free comfort zone left her feeling frustrated and trapped.

If Tina's story resonates with you, ask yourself why. Once you solve that riddle, you'll be on the way to a more fulfilling personal and professional life.

"Love isn't always on time." —Toto
"Chemistry isn't always on time." —Me

I have new business meetings all the time, and I never know how they're going to go. But one "get to know you" in late 2019 felt like the biggest dud ever.

Brenda led an upstart med-tech company. She was a nice person, and I could sense her leadership qualities. But we had no business chemistry, so I did something bold.

"Brenda, we're not connecting here," I said midway through our breakfast. "Why don't we save ourselves some time and cut this one short?"

If Brenda was offended, she hid it well. We parted ways amicably, and that was that. Except it wasn't.

To my surprise, Brenda emailed me later that day and told me how much she respected my decision to end our meeting. She admitted that she didn't feel any chemistry with me, either, and she appreciated my lack of Minnesota passive-aggressiveness.

Ironically, this email created the first spark of chemistry between us. Suddenly, I *did* want to work with Brenda. I knew from our small talk that she was passionate about cooking, so I got an idea. I went online, found a set of high-end kitchen knives and had her initials etched into them. I wrote her a personal letter to go with the gift, and I included the best quotes I could find on the similarities between cooking and leadership.

This move carried a certain amount of risk. I knew that Brenda was into cooking, but I didn't know how she would interpret my gesture. She could have found it too forward, or even creepy. I mean, who was I to assume that I "got" her after one meeting—especially one that I chose to cut short? I ignored that voice, trusted my instincts and sent the gift anyway.

Brenda called me as soon as she got it.

"This is the nicest thing anyone has ever sent me!" she said. "I want you to meet our CMO." Her company became a Media Bridge client, and Brenda has become a valuable colleague.

The moral of the story is that sometimes chemistry doesn't strike right away. We're used to the Hollywood version where a metaphorical lightning bolt instantly transforms two people. The truth is far less dramatic: sometimes you have to be patient and give chemistry a nudge.

It's also about the importance of simply listening to people and caring about them. I took enough of a personal interest in Brenda to ask what she was passionate about and remember it later. She wasn't a client. She wasn't a friend. She was a complete stranger that I was having breakfast with. But I was still curious to learn as much as I could about her, and that opened a door.

We all know the saying "You make your own luck." It's about doing the hard work and putting yourself in a position to take advantage of luck when it happens. Chemistry is the same way. You can't always expect it to happen with no work on your part. But if you're willing to nurture it, you can make it happen.

False Chemistry

Years ago, I met a passionate entrepreneur in the credit repair business we'll call Nick. I audited Nick's media spending and showed him how Media Bridge could deliver more bang for his advertising buck. He quickly became one of our biggest accounts.

My chemistry with Nick was off the charts. We made a great team. I loved his high risk tolerance and aggressive approach to media. He trusted me completely, let me do what I do best and basically said yes to everything I recommended. Before long, Nick's company was beating its competitors and expanding into new markets. He looked unstoppable.

Until the IRS raided his offices.

Nick insisted to me that he'd done nothing wrong. I not only believed him, I defended him to my friends, colleagues and other clients. I even introduced him to a crisis PR firm to help him navigate his negative publicity. I had his back no matter what.

The scales finally fell from my eyes when Nick stopped paying his bills while insisting that I keep his media plan running. That meant tons of money out of my pocket and none out of his. *No, thank you*, I thought. *There's a word for that: stealing.*

Like a jilted lover, I did a 180 on my relationship with Nick. I cut off his media plan. I refused to take his calls. I took him to court, and I won. Shocker, he didn't pay me. As I write this, he sits in a jail cell and still owes me money.

Does this story sound familiar? Of course it does. Personally and professionally, we've all fallen for the wrong person at some point. If we're honest about it, we've probably done it multiple times. Your friends try to warn you that the toxic person you're dating or working with is bad for you. "You're crazy!" you say. "You don't know him like I do!" You felt the chemistry so strongly early on. How could it be lying to you now?

If you're lucky, something eventually happens that crosses a line with your conscience and exposes the truth. When this happens, you go back to your friends and put your failure on *them*.

"Why didn't you slap me across the face and insist that I break up with that horrible person?"

"I tried," they say. "But it's like you were hypnotized."

People told me not to trust Nick, and I didn't listen to them. The writing was on the wall, and I ignored every word until our relationship ended in theft and betrayal. It happens in life. It happens in business.

So how can you tell when the chemistry you feel with someone is the wrong kind? It's not easy, and I'm still working on it. I've gotten better at recognizing when my stubborn loyalty to a person is rooted in denial, or not wanting to admit that I'm wrong. And I know that I can feel exaggerated chemistry in a new relationship if I feel burned by the one that came right before it.

The Core Values Chemistry Test

Because chemistry is so emotion-based, it helps to create an objective measure of it that gives you an outside perspective when you need it. Core values serve that purpose in my business life, and I recommend that every person discover their own.

Core values get a bad rap because they're so often seen as an obligation, a box to check. This mindset results in CEOs throwing words like "Integrity" and "Persistence" on posters in the cafeteria and expecting them to take hold in their company culture by osmosis.

I, on the other hand, have become obsessed with core values. You can ask my 50+ employees at Media Bridge. I expect everyone to know them and live by them every day, especially me. We have three:

1. Lead with Heart
2. Raise the Bar
3. Do the Right Thing

Each of these values is authentic to our agency. Each expresses who we are and where we want to go, both as people and as a company. Each Media Bridge employee can recite them on the spot. And when we gather for quarterly State of the Company meetings, we start by recognizing our colleagues who have demonstrated our core values over the last three months.

We also use our core values to hire and fire. Whenever something feels "off" with a client or employee, our values provide a touchstone that helps us define the problem and decide how to deal with it. If I had worked this way during the Nick relationship, I would have seen that he never led with heart or did the right thing. He was actually a master manipulator driven by greed. He saw people as a means to an end.

Business chemistry can create a powerful electrical current. But when someone's actions don't feel right, core values can provide the circuit breaker that snaps you back to reality. Your core values should be unique to you and your business. Never make an important decision without consulting them.

Afterglow

We often get into bed with lovers the same way we get into business with colleagues. It's all about the chemistry we feel or don't feel. Be open to feeling connection with other people in all facets of life, but also understand your unique relationship to chemistry. Sometimes it's instant; other times it requires patience. It can be healthy and fulfilling, or it can be self-destructive. To expose false chemistry, figure out your core values and constantly measure yourself and the people you meet against them.

5 Questions

1. Are you open to feeling chemistry with other people in your personal life, or do you shut yourself off out of fear of rejection?

2. If you feel a lack of chemistry with your current romantic partner, do you also feel it with your current job or career?

3. Do you have a pattern of "false chemistry" in your personal and/or professional life? Are you frequently drawn to people who wind up being toxic?

4. Can you think of a case in your personal or professional life when you didn't feel chemistry with someone right away, but did later?

5. What are your top three core values? What traits do you try to demonstrate as a person and an organization, and do you insist that others demonstrate them as well?

Your "Chemistry Network"

Chemistry is best when it's shared. That's why I often play matchmaker by bringing people together in my chemistry network.

I could fill a chapter with the times I've introduced clients to organizations that have become valuable business partners for them. I could also write a book about a program I offer to Media Bridge employees called MB Dreams: I sit down with team members one-on-one, help them discover what they're most passionate about, then connect them with people who can help them on that journey. It's been a huge success and the most fulfilling part of my job as a leader.

My business has also benefited from others' chemistry networks. From a new business standpoint, cold-calling and answering RFPs is like going to the bar and having no idea what you're going to get. Some of our best leads have come from existing clients setting us up with their friends in the same industry. It works because these referrals are chemistry "pre-approved."

For example, our work with local Midwestern mega real estate agent Kris Lindahl led to work with his friend Gary Ashton, who leads the most successful RE/MAX team in the world from his headquarters in Nashville. And our work with an industry group called Medical Alley has led to a growing list of med-tech clients.

Whether you've thought about it or not, you probably have a strong chemistry network of your own. Recognize it as one of your most valuable tools. If you use it to help others, the karma will come back to you many times over.

Chapter 4: The Lesbian Advantage

*"Men who fantasize about lesbian sex don't
realize it's just two women in a room saying,
'No YOU come first. No, YOU!' till they self-combust."*

—Tig Notaro

Early in my media career, I worked with a lot of car dealers, all straight men. One in particular would ask me to go to strip clubs with him. It might sound weird that a guy would invite a female media rep to join him to gawk at naked women, especially since he was married. You're probably assuming that I was creeped out or offended by it, and that he hid these visits from his wife. Neither is true. His wife knew me, knew that I was a lesbian and knew that her husband went to strip clubs. She was fine with it. In fact, she preferred that he go with me instead of with his guy friends.

This story has played out dozens of times in my career: straight men feel more freedom around me once they learn my sexuality. I call it "The Lesbian Advantage," and while it's not *always* an advantage, it does say a lot about business, sexual dynamics and the nature of intimacy.

Sexy Business Secret #4

Business and sex both revolve around relationships.
But in business, you can achieve more intimacy
when you take sex out of the equation.

One of the Guys. Sort Of.

I'm a realist about sex. When you find someone physically attractive and spend enough time with them, things inevitably turn sexual. It happens at the bar. It happens in the office. How many people have you known who weren't initially attracted to each other, then ended up doing the four-legged fox trot after going on a business trip? Maybe you're one of them. Heck, maybe that's how you met your partner!

That simply doesn't happen with me and men, and attraction with no chance of sex is awesome. Men never have to think that I'm hitting on them or snubbing them. And they know that I'm not rejecting *them* sexually; I'm rejecting *all* men sexually. "It's nothing personal," I say. "You just don't have the right parts!"

> "I also have the advantage of being one of the guys, yet not one of the guys. Men will confide in me more than they will with their closest guy friends."

I'm a touchy person. I like to hug people, walk arm in arm with them, give them a peck on the cheek or lips. Straight men like that physical connection with a woman. With no sexual tension, my straight male business partners, colleagues and employees and I have total freedom to travel, go to bars on weekends and have as many late-night gab sessions as we want. They don't have to "check in" as often. Their wives don't worry that they'll cross a line. And I can touch a man on his arm and not feel like I have to pull my hand back when someone walks into the room.

I also have the advantage of being one of the guys, yet not one of the guys. Men will confide in me more than they will with their closest guy friends. If it's just the two of us, there's less pressure to be a "guy's guy" and more space to be honest and vulnerable about their professional and personal lives.

Similarly, being a lesbian also gives me an advantage with straight women. These women often compete with each other for men's attention, as well as for advancement in most professional cultures. (For more on this, see Chapter 7: "Men Suck & Women Cut.") Once again, I don't present a threat in this scenario. Like straight men, straight women feel an added freedom to be themselves around me. Before long, I'm hearing secrets that they haven't even shared with their spouses.

I wish it didn't have to be this way. I wish everyone felt free to be open with everyone else regardless of their gender or sexuality. But unfortunately, that's not the case … yet.

Achieving Your Own "Lesbian Advantage"

"That's great for you, Tracy," you might be thinking if you're a straight woman. "But what about me?" Fair question.

Straight women can achieve the Lesbian Advantage with gay men. But this is about more than simply saying "straight person + gay person = ideal business relationship." The bigger point is that in business, you achieve the greatest intimacy when you remove sexual possibilities.

Conscious and unconscious sexual dynamics are constantly at play in our work lives. That's just a fact. Finding a way to build a relationship that isn't wrapped up in sexuality requires you to find something you have in common with someone—something that builds nonsexual chemistry.

In my case, activating my lesbianism with a straight man builds an instant wall and opens a door at the same time, so it's easier. If you're a straight woman dealing with straight men, you have a harder job. But it's possible. Every nonsexual bond I have with a straight male client can also be a bond between a straight woman and a straight man. With one client, our bond is leadership. With another, it's the fact that we grew up as only children. With another, it's our shared passion for dogs. What's your advantage?

The Big Reveal

I just used the term "activating my lesbianism." You might wonder how I do this. I mean, how do clients and colleagues even know my sexuality? It's not like I wear a red "Make America Lesbian Again" baseball cap.

Today, people can google me and learn that I'm gay before they meet me. They can pull up an article from the *Minneapolis/ St. Paul Business Journal* about how I made their "Business of Pride" list in 2019. They can learn that I founded Minnesotans for Equality 2012 and partnered with former Minnesota Vikings punter Chris Kluwe to help defeat a bill outlawing same-sex marriage in Minnesota.

I don't draw attention to my sexuality directly. Doing that can sound like a disclaimer or a trigger warning. "Just so you know, I'm a lesbian" flies in the face of everything my community stands for. Instead, my policy is to be myself, just like everybody else. When a male client mentions his wife and kids, so do I. It's that simple.

After that, it's all about their reaction. If someone clams up when I say "my wife," then I know we might not be a good fit. Sometimes I'll ignore the awkward pause. Other times I'll call it out—but not in an aggressive way, and never in a group setting. When we're away from others, I'll say, "Am I imagining things, or did you have a physical reaction when I said 'my wife'? Maybe I misread you, but that's who I am, and it's too early in our relationship to have a problem. Do you want to talk about it?"

Sometimes they'll deny it, then they'll ghost me later. I'll do some digital research of my own and discover why. When you're gay, it's easy to sniff out homophobia online, both in terms of what people do and don't post.

The Lesbian Disadvantage

And that brings me to the counter-argument to the title of this chapter. While I do enjoy some advantages in my business relationships, I don't want to give the impression that being a lesbian in a business world still dominated by straight men is all positive. I also don't want to minimize or trivialize the harassment that straight women deal with. No one's sexuality should work against them. I'm fortunate that I don't have to deal with male harassment to the same degree that straight women do.

But I still deal with some nonsense, like straight men claiming that I'm "not really a lesbian" or that they can "flip" me. Most of these guys get the message when I shoot them down once, but I've learned that you can't joke away their comments or let them off the hook with a smile. Today, I say, "You know what? That's actually not funny; it's offensive." Then I laugh on the inside, because these guys think I've never had sex with a man. I have, and no thank you!

The upside of being "one of the guys" is that straight men will be more honest and vulnerable with you. The downside is that sometimes the locker room talk slips out. A man in a professional group I belong to once used the term "wifebeater" to refer to a white tank top. In the past, I would have let the comment slide. But this time, I took him aside and said, "You know, using that term really makes you sound out of touch. What if there was a woman in the room who was getting beaten by her husband or boyfriend?"

The realization washed over his face. He didn't get mad or defensive. He appreciated what I'd done, and he thanked me. Sometimes you can turn disadvantage back into advantage. Speaking of that …

Conversion Therapy

Mike McGuire was one of my first clients at Media Bridge. A rep at a local radio station introduced us because his growing franchise business needed a more sophisticated media buyer. When I called him to meet for coffee, Mike said, "I don't drink coffee. I drink beer." Translation: "I'm a man's man."

I knew exactly what to do. I met Mike at 9 a.m. at one of his storefronts, armed with a six-pack of Bud Light. We sat on his counter and drank it while we talked about life and business and sports, and we've worked together ever since. A few years later, Mike was one of two straight men who read my vows for me when I married Pam. I'm sure he never anticipated going to a lesbian wedding, let alone participating in one. But he did, and the world is a better place because of it.

Mike is just one example of how being a lesbian has helped me forge meaningful friendships with people I share little in common with. We don't hang out in the same social circles. We don't consume the same news sources. We don't vote the same. Under different circumstances, we would never be friends. But we are, and I'm grateful for that.

Now when I see Mike, I give him a great big smooch. He's like family to me, to the point where we can be incredibly direct— even confrontational—and still be friends. That's extremely rare today, and I consider it a gift.

Know what else is a gift? The fact that when it comes to the "I can flip you" guys, more often than not, I actually flip *them* into being more accepting of people who aren't like them. Ironic, isn't it?

Afterglow

Sex is an intimate act, but in business, intimacy comes from eliminating sexual tension. Being a lesbian has allowed me to quickly forge deep friendships with straight men and women. I still have to deal with people who don't accept me as "normal" or who think they can change me, but trends are moving in the right direction. If you're a straight woman in a male-dominated business culture, the best way to shut off sexual tension and open the door to deeper relationships with male clients and colleagues is to connect in a nonsexual way. You don't have to become a "sexless" person. You just have to find nonsexual common interests.

5 Questions

1. Do you feel that your gender and sexuality currently enhance or hinder your professional relationships and advancement?

2. What's the strongest nonsexual bond you've felt with a client or colleague?

3. Have you ever felt competitive with another woman for the attention of a man at work?

4. Does sexual tension underlie that competitiveness, and do you feel like you need to use your sexuality (say, by flirting) to "win" the competition?

5. When the possibility of sex with another person is 100% off the table, do you feel more or less "free" with them?

PART III:
DOING THE DEED

Let's talk about finding the G spot.

That place of happiness, bliss and ecstasy.

If you have good sex, then you probably have

good business too. If you don't, then why not?

Chapter 5: Finding the G Spot

"My sex life is so bad, my G spot has been declared a historical landmark."

—Joan Rivers

Let's clear up one thing right now: unlike Bigfoot, the Loch Ness monster and "reverse racism," the G spot is real. Wikipedia describes its existence as "unproven," but screw that. I've found it hundreds (thousands?) of times with dozens of people. I've literally taken women's hands and shown them where it is on me. It's a real place on the actual vaginal wall. End of story.

People who question the G spot's existence are usually straight men, but that's because they've never found it. For lesbians, it's kinda your most important thing, so we're more knowledgeable (and persistent). So if you're a man who thinks the G spot is as fictional as Santa Claus, you're wrong. It's real, and it's the gift that keeps on giving.

Sexy Business Secret #5

Every person has a different personal and professional G spot. A good businesswoman knows how to find them.

Literal and Figurative G Spots

I was once driving to a meeting with a coworker (call him Jon) when our conversation veered into interesting territory:

Jon: I'm not sure if I should ask you this question.

Me: Must be a good one. Try me.

Jon: Is there really such a thing as a G spot?

Me: (Trying not to spit out my coffee) Of course there is!

Jon: Then how come I've never been able to find the damn thing?

Me: It can be hard to find if you don't know when and where to explore. Wait, aren't you engaged?

Jon: Yeah.

Me: Jon, that's a problem.

Jon: I know. So how do I solve it? It's not like they teach you how to find a G spot in health class.

Me: Here's the deal. It's not exactly the same with every woman, but it's in the same general area. You have to go in a few inches and curl your fingers. It's usually where your middle finger is. It's about the size of a nickel, and if the timing is right, it feels a little rough.

Jon wasn't following me, so I took his hand and slipped it into his dashboard cassette tape player.

Me: Now curl your fingers until you feel something sharp.

Jon: Ow!

Me: Bingo!

Jon wasn't happy that I made him prick his finger, but he soon forgot about it. The next time I saw him at work, he had a huge smile on his face.

Sexually, the G spot is tangible. In a business context, it exists in a figurative sense that's no less powerful. It's where your clients and colleagues feel seen, heard, understood and cared for. It's the place that feels professionally orgasmic.

My friend Tina suffered from a chronic lack of joy because she wasn't finding the figurative G spot in her career, and her partner wasn't finding the real one on her. Millions of women feel the same way: their professional frustration mirrors their sexual frustration. If you're one of those people, then this is your lucky day.

Everyone's Different

My friend Jaque Bethke is a genius architect, engineer and interior designer. She works with people and businesses all over the world. Her superpower is that whenever she walks into a space, visions of what it should look like flood her brain. These visions are a mix of her personal tastes and her clients' unique personalities, so they come from a combination of creativity and empathy.

I can't do what Jaque does, but I have a similar superpower when it comes to people: I can sense their energy in a heightened way, and I know how to make it more positive. In pitch meetings, I let others present so I can focus on the body language around the table. I can think what people are thinking. I can feel what they're feeling. I can sense when they need attention and what kind of attention they need.

> To be a good lover, you have to be in the moment and totally tuned in, but you also have to note how your partner reacts to different moves in different moments.

My ability to see people's potential is a superpower that applies both in the office and at home, to the point where my son thinks I'm clairvoyant. As you might expect, it also applies in bed. To be a good lover, you have to be in the moment and totally tuned in, but you also have to note how your partner reacts to different moves in different moments. I feel my partner's *energy* as well as her body. I sense when I need to go faster or slower, stay where I am or go someplace else, use more pressure or less. I've been with women who like it hard and fast and crazy. I've been with others who like it soft and slow. Everybody's different.

Similarly, my clients, colleagues and employees each have their own "business G spots." One client likes it most when you take everything off her plate and say, "Don't worry, we'll handle it." Another one needs you to listen deeply to him because most people can't keep up with his intense mind. Still another is new to being a CEO and craves advice on leadership.

My favorite example is two entrepreneurial clients I've worked with who are in the same industry, but in different parts of the country. They're both phenomenally successful, but their business G spots are as far apart as their headquarters. One craves attention and engagement. The other needs sympathy and understanding. One wants everything hot, heavy, fast and furious, then wants his back scratched. The other wants it slow and deliberate, or maybe he just wants to hang out for a while and escape the daily grind.

My employees are just as diverse. Some of them like it when you're direct and blunt. Others are more sensitive and thrive on praise and nurturing. One of my former leadership team members loved it when I would hug her and tell her how amazing she was. Another didn't like to be touched, but she had a figurative orgasm every time I brought her a fresh croissant from her favorite restaurant.

"What about results and ROI?" you might be thinking. "Isn't that the real business G spot for every client?" Not as much as you'd think. Our clients expect (and receive) more clicks and customers when they work with Media Bridge. Tactically, their business G spot could be their media mix or a certain marketing message. We might know one radio station in a certain market that always spikes leads, or one piece of creative that consistently boosts ROI whenever we go back to it.

But on a more personal level, our clients' business G spots have nothing to do with their bottom lines. Some don't even look at their cost-per-lead reports. It's more about how we work with them. Some prefer to talk in the morning, when they have a clearer head and make better decisions. Others would rather talk late at night when they feel less tense. Some develop better ideas on their home turf; others think more outside the box when we get them off site, maybe to a happy hour. Some want a dog-and-pony show when we present a media plan or a creative campaign. Others just want a one-sheet telling them exactly what they need to do and when.

Would our clients walk away if we failed to deliver results? Absolutely. But what gets them off is more emotional. It's "getting between the spreadsheets."

Giving vs. Receiving

A few years ago, my wife Pam gave me a custom coupon book filled with items like "3 Free Hugs!" and "Good for 1 Foot Massage!" It was a loving gesture. She gave it to me because I tend to put others' needs ahead of my own. Today, it's sitting in a landfill or has been recycled into a cardboard box for Amazon. I never used it.

Like many of you reading this book, I'm not great at telling people what I need. In my case, it's for two reasons: once I say what I want at the beginning of a relationship, I expect my partner to remember it forever. And I get off on getting other people off more than I get off on them getting me off. (That's a lot of "getting offs," but you get the idea.)

These reasons are problematic. The first one is unfair. We all have different superpowers. Just because I'm hyper-attuned to sensing what others need doesn't give me the right to expect others to be the same way. As for the second one, sometimes I *do* like to receive pleasure more than giving it. I just have a hard time admitting it.

I encourage our Media Bridge team to express their needs, wants and desires on a regular basis. And we've built systems to make that easy and safe for them. But like many people, I suck at implementing those ideas in my personal life. I'll occasionally ask Pam for a foot rub. I'll sometimes walk up to her and say, "Meet me in the bedroom in five minutes." But in general, I expect others to read me as well as I read them. And that's not fair.

Another case in point: I've built a multimillion-dollar company largely on my skills as a media negotiator and my ability to hire others with the same talent, but I'm terrible at negotiating for myself. I'll fight to the death to make sure that every penny of our clients' budgets works as hard as possible for them. Friends will ask me to help them negotiate better deals with their employers, clients, even their cable companies. But when I plan a vacation, I'll pay full price for every part of it because I don't like to haggle on my own behalf.

In both sex and business, the most difficult balance to achieve is "giving" vs. "receiving." For example, many people love to talk about "grit," especially men. "Don't stop, won't stop!" they say. In both business and sex, they feel like they need to keep pumping away. *Harder, faster, harder, faster!* It's all about them.

But once you understand giving—once you learn what it really takes to give your partner an orgasm or build a healthy and sustainable business, then you realize how nuanced it really is. You learn to work smarter, not harder. You learn to slow down, then go fast, then slow down again. Vary the speed. Change the rhythm. Shift the intensity.

On the flip (mostly female) side, business professionals love to quote the airline safety mantra: "Put the oxygen mask on yourself before giving it to others." You're of no use to anyone if you're dead—that's easy to understand. But what many women need to hear is that you also can't deliver pleasure to another person if you don't allow *yourself* to feel it as well. Most women don't communicate what's working and not working sexually with their partners, then they get frustrated when the sex feels one-sided. Part of that is *your* responsibility. You have to communicate.

As for me, I still feel better when I give than when I receive. I still would rather give a big orgasm than receive one. And I still get more satisfaction from seeing our clients make the Inc. 5000 list than from us making it. But I also know—as should you—that giving is a problem if you don't let yourself receive.

Don't Get Taken for Granted

In business and in life, women generally don't like to brag about their efforts and accomplishments. This creates a vicious cycle. When people don't know what you do for them, they're free to take you for granted.

The same principle applies in business. An example from my industry: a big part of media buying is "reconciliation," or making sure every ad runs exactly as it's supposed to, then holding media companies accountable to make up for mistakes (e.g., if the local TV station didn't run your commercial before the weather report on their local newscast last Wednesday because they ran out of time, then they'd better run it this Wednesday).

Reconciliation is a time-consuming process that media agencies generally can't charge for, so many don't put much effort into it. Media plans can be sprawling and complex. If a client isn't aware of one mistake on one day at one station in one market, then it didn't really happen, right?

Wrong. I can't stand it when someone doesn't get exactly what they've paid for (and what my team has meticulously negotiated for on their behalf), so Media Bridge pays people full-time to lose us money in the short term through reconciliation. The effort is worth it to me for three reasons: it's the right thing to do, it builds trust, and it makes more money in the long term. In the past, we didn't always communicate our reconciliation process to our clients, so they didn't know the value we were delivering. We've changed that.

When you find the G spot during sex, your partner can't help but feel it. When you find the G spot in business, sometimes you have to let people know about it.

Afterglow

The G spot is literally real in sex and figuratively real in business. In both realms, it's different for each person. It's not always easy to find. And yours won't be accessible to others unless you're open, honest, confident and vulnerable. If you're lacking orgasms in your sex life, then you're probably lacking joy in your career as well. The good news is this: once you do find the G spot in one part of your life, the other part usually follows.

5 Questions

1. When it comes to sex and business, are you more of a giver or a receiver?

2. Do you feel appreciated at home and at work, or taken for granted?

3. Do you know what gets each of your colleagues, employees and clients off, or do you tend to treat them all the same?

4. Similarly, do you let people know what your figurative G spot is at work, or do you just expect them to know?

5. In general, do you feel more responsible for pleasing others than for receiving pleasure yourself?

Smaller Can Be Better

Having a big one isn't always a good thing. I'm talking about businesses, not penises or clitorises (clitori?). Actually, I'm talking about genitals, too. I once knew a guy whose penis was so big that he had a hard time getting women to sleep with him. But I digress ...

Actually, let's roll with that. In my industry, sometimes a big agency is like a big penis: it's too much, and it's not a good fit. Some entrepreneurs and CEOs think that working with a "big agency" is a rite of passage that means they've made it.

But in advertising and many other industries, the smaller players are often better at delivering what their clients need. In other words, they're better at finding their professional G spot.

As of this writing, my Media Bridge team has grown to over 50 people. That's still far from being a "big agency," and I love it. Instead of pretending that we're a multinational conglomerate that can meet every marketing need for every client, I'll often surprise potential clients by calling us the "un-full-service agency." We do what we're great at and let others do the rest.

In a world where many agencies claim to specialize in everything (impossible by definition), I deliver a radically against-the-grain message that emphasizes our limits. Admitting that you're *not* all things to all people is a sign of strength, not weakness. People love the candor, and they want to work with you even more.

Chapter 6:
One-Night Stands
vs. True Connection

"Guess it's true, I'm not good at a one-night stand
But I still need love 'cause I'm just a man
These nights never seem to go to plan
I don't want you to leave, will you hold my hand?
Darling, stay with me."

—Sam Smith

Fifteen years after Ian said "don't kiss me back" in that Iowa State stairwell, I seduced the woman who is now my wife by using a variation on his theme.

I knew about the legendary Pam Kosanke, but I had never met her. Like me, she was a driven marketing professional and an athlete (we both played rugby). Like me, she was a control freak with an intense personality. And like me, she liked women. So when I heard that she was traveling to Minneapolis from Chicago for a mutual friend's wedding, I offered to put her up at my house.

"Don't stay with Tracy unless you're prepared to wind up in bed with her," our mutual friend had warned Pam. "You two have way too much in common." She was right. Pam and I were destined to either love or hate each other. And soon. Because Pam accepted my invitation.

From the moment I met Pam at the airport, I had that "something is going to happen" feeling. I had also felt it with Ian, but he was my opposite. Pam and I were a perfect match. When we arrived at my house and she set her bag down in my kitchen, I looked at this impossibly beautiful, strong and brilliant woman and could no longer contain myself.

Ian's opening move to me was a cool "come here" gesture. I wasn't so subtle with Pam. I walked up to her, picked her up and set her on my kitchen counter. Then, as I stood between her legs, I started not kissing her. That's right, *not* kissing her. As if by instinct, Pam joined in, and it became a dance. Our faces moved in and out, hovered around each other. Our cheeks grazed; our lips barely brushed. It was the ultimate tease. We'd later call it "kissing without kissing," and it was better than kissing. The energy. The heat. By trying so hard not to touch each other, every accidental touch became explosive.

The restraint couldn't last forever, of course. The dam broke in a big way later that day and throughout the weekend. Everything about it is still fresh in my mind. I can still see the light streaming into my bedroom. I can still feel the heat of the early summer sun on my body. I can still smell the lilacs just outside my open window.

I knew the truth immediately: this was no one-night stand. Pam and I connected so intensely—physically, intellectually and in every other way possible—that we soon decided to bottle those feelings forever. We've been happily married since 2014.

Sexy Business Secret #6

*Like the G spot, one-night stands are literal in
sex and figurative in business. No judgment.
Both have their place, depending on what each party is
looking for. The important thing is knowing the
difference and not mistaking one for the other.*

What Exactly Is a "One-Night Stand"?

I have no right to be snooty about booty calls. If you count makeout sessions, I've had hundreds of "hit and runs." One night in college, I literally went floor to floor in a frat house and made out with a different guy in each room.

I didn't go all the way with any of them because sex has always been a big line for me. I can talk a big game, but I'm pretty turfy about letting people into my pants. Despite what you might be thinking at this point based on my openness about sex, my number of sexual partners (8–10) is statistically average. Seriously, I just googled it. I'm "normal"!

> "In business, one-night stands are everywhere."

The problem with one-night stands is that they can be deceiving. You're usually drunk. Everyone seems more attractive to you than they really are. You mash. Then you replay everything the next day and regret it. In the end, the experience feels hollow and doesn't leave you with anything meaningful.

In business, one-night stands are everywhere. In my industry, the best example is when media companies execute cookie-cutter national media buys for clients who don't even need them. They buy ad space on TV and radio stations from Phoenix to Philadelphia when the company doesn't even do business in Phoenix or Philadelphia. It looks sexy. It's lots of money and media impressions on paper. But it's a ridiculously inefficient strategy. In short, it's a one-night stand. After the initial rush, both parties wake up the next morning with a hangover and think, "Did we even have a connection?"

Ever taken a job that looked sexy, then turned out to be the most miserable experience of your life? Before you know it, you're doing the corporate Walk of Shame and carrying a box of your belongings back to your car. That's a one-night stand.

Ever gone into business with a partner who looked like a great fit as you signed the letters of incorporation, then turned out to be difficult, unethical, lazy or incompetent once you got into day-to-day operations with them? One-night stand.

Ever done business with a client who gave your revenue a quick jolt but didn't fit your business model, then proceeded to strain your relationships with better business partners? One. Night. Stand.

Why Do One-Night Stands Happen?

One-night stands can be fun, but often they're misguided attempts to mask pain or fill a void. Maybe you're on the rebound. Maybe you're getting back at a partner who broke up with you. Maybe you think getting drunk and sleeping with someone will bring back your sexual confidence. Or maybe you're just horny and it's been a while.

In business, one-night stands happen when you're misled, you fail to read someone's true intentions or you're desperate to keep the cash flow going. They also happen when you enter into a relationship too fast and fail to align your expectations.

I've seen countless one-night stands in advertising where the agency doesn't take enough time to learn the client's long-term goals and what has (or hasn't) worked in the past. The agency throws together recommendations without the data to justify them. Then they buy airtime, billboards and digital ads without knowing the key performance indicators that will define success. Predictably, the relationship ends when the campaign fails to deliver results.

People who are happy and fulfilled in their personal and professional lives aren't the one-night stand types. They think long term. They focus on building and maintaining relationships. They're loyal. Instead of grabbing quick fixes, they seek a consistent feeling of happiness, well-being and growth.

In other words, they have:

A Bigger Purpose

As I made my way up the media-buying ladder in Minneapolis, I heard one name over and over again: Anne Gallagher. No one was more respected than Anne. Advertisers loved her. Media companies loved her. Everybody looked up to her. It wasn't just her high volume of buys or the revenue she brought in. When people talked about her, they used words like "professional," "trusted," "fair" and "integrity."

To be honest, I was kind of an asshole when I started in the business. Buying media requires you to make different groups of people happy. It's a delicate dance. You represent the advertiser, so you need to deliver the biggest bang for their media buck. But the media companies are also your partners. They won't work with you if they don't like you, and if they won't work with you, then neither will the advertisers. It's a three-way relationship. (Note to self: write a chapter on "sex and business three-ways" for the sequel to this book.)

I acted like a sports agent early in my career. In that world, you only have to make the player happy, because the team has no choice but to work with you. It was a one-night stand because I focused too much on the advertisers and not enough on the media who attracted their customers. I was good at playing hardball. Too good. Eventually, my ego got in the way. I pushed too hard, and I learned hard lessons in return. I eventually decided that I wanted true connection. I wanted to be like Anne Gallagher.

After I righted my ship and earned the trust and respect I wanted, a funny thing happened: it felt so good that I kept on going. Over time—and through heavy doses of education, networking, counseling and coaching—I've discovered that my mission in life is *connection*. I need to feel connected to people psychologically, mentally and emotionally. And I thrive on connecting people with each other.

Based on this insight, I started the MB Dreams program that I mentioned earlier. When you're on Team Media Bridge, it's not enough for me to know your professional skills. I want to know what makes you tick as a human being, and connect the dots to help you get what you really want out of life. Maybe I can help you finance a project. Maybe I can introduce you to people in my Chemistry Network. In one case, I befriended a political candidate based on a team member's passion for social justice. We produced a video for her political race, then we watched her become the first Black Muslim woman ever elected to serve in the Minnesota Senate.

As an entrepreneur, I have a bigger mission than making money. I want to make an impact and leave a legacy. When I'm done with Media Bridge, I want people to feel that they learned and grew by working with me. When I'm done with life, I want people to feel that they learned and grew by having me as a friend, mom, wife and colleague. That's not a one-night stand; that's true connection.

Afterglow

On their deathbeds, few people say, "I wish I had worked more." Even fewer say, "I wish I'd had more one-night stands." Yet many of us operate with a daily mindset that takes us from one hookup to another, both personally and professionally. Then we wonder why we feel empty. In the end, we only remember our deepest relationships—to people, places, experiences and ideas. We think of that family member, neighbor, teacher, coach, colleague or boss who changed our life because they listened, saw something in us and took the time to help us.

5 Questions

1. Do your personal and romantic relationships tend to be short-term or long-term?

2. Do you show the same pattern in your job and career?

3. Are you someone who truly wants to find a job that you're 100% committed to, or do you feel the need to keep your options open?

4. Some people look back and realize that a one-night stand was actually one of the best connections they ever made with another person. Have you ever had a one-night stand that could have grown into a longer relationship?

5. Has the same thing ever happened with a job? You took its benefits for granted and left for something better, then later regretted it?

The Second Orgasm

Much is made of the first orgasm, but orgasm #2 is actually better. Shorter and harder to earn, yes, but also way more intense. (Some men reading this are fascinated by the idea of a second orgasm. They're usually snoring after the first one.)

In business, second meetings are like second orgasms. First meetings are easy. Everyone's excited and on their best behavior. You're just getting to know each other. People listen intently, do their best to impress each other, then sometimes forget everything the minute they walk out the door.

The first meeting and first orgasm are the discovery phase. You don't "close" anyone. The second go-round is when you show true connection and prove that you know what you're doing.

In both situations, you look for the moments when the other person (or *people,* for my polyamorous peeps) lights up. In bed, it's when your partner leans forward, arches their back and moans. In business, it's when a client shuts her laptop, snaps to attention and gets excited about new possibilities. Either way, it's a sign to go deeper.

Everyone expects a first meeting to go well in business. It's the second one that closes the deal. In sex, greater pleasure often comes the second time around, as do the people involved.

Making a Move

I was madly in love with Cass, but I couldn't tell if she felt the same way about me. She lived in a neighboring dorm and worked as a security officer in mine, and I would go out of my way to "bump into" her as often as possible. But I never made the first move.

I was bold and brave with men, but I lacked confidence with Cass because I hadn't been with a woman yet. Even after I came out, she never said anything about our flirtation. I even helped her and her wife buy a house years later when I worked as a real estate agent.

When I recently told a mutual friend of ours that Cass was my first crush, he blurted out, "Oh my God, she just told me the same thing about you!" I was floored. At a Minneapolis Pride event soon after that, Cass and I saw each other and talked about our college past. Back then, I thought she found me annoying. She told me she didn't. She thought I was straight. I wasn't.

We laugh about it now, but in that moment, we regretted that we had missed an opportunity out of fear and false assumptions. Maybe we would have had a one-night stand. Maybe we would have felt a deeper connection. We never got to experience either.

When personal and professional relationship problems mirror each other, it often comes down to an inability to ask for what you want. Maybe you don't actually know what you want. Maybe you don't have the confidence to ask for it. Maybe you don't feel like you deserve it. Maybe it's all three.

Making a Move (cont.)

Professionally, people refuse to make the first move in dozens of areas: quitting their jobs, starting new careers, challenging their bosses, exploring ideas others might not like. It's the same with sex. How many times have you sat on the couch next to your partner and thought, "I want to have sex. It's been too long. But I don't want to make the first move. I'm tired. I haven't taken a shower. Besides, they might say no."

I can't tell you what's going to happen if you finally make that move you've been avoiding, but I can tell you what will happen if you don't: nothing.

Make the first move.

Chapter 7: Men Suck & Women Cut

Middle-aged man: *If I don't get paid to say whatever
I want wherever I want it, I am
oppressed.*

Woman: **Apologizes to a chair for bumping
into it.*

—Tweet from @JenAshleyWright

My wife Pam is a rock star marketer. She's managed huge accounts at big ad agencies. She's served as a CEO, CMO and CRO at male-dominated nonprofits, entrepreneurial companies and corporations with private-equity ownership. Everywhere she's worked, she's operated at a pace that few others can keep up with, and she's consistently delivered impressive results. Yet she still feels like she has to be twice as qualified and work twice as hard as her male colleagues.

I know the feeling, as does every woman reading this book.

The business world is still dominated by men, and an invisible (and sometimes visible) system works to maintain that power structure. Men favor other men, give each other the "benefit of the doubt" when things go wrong, award business contracts to old college buddies, and focus on "potential" and "upside" with their male job applicants vs. "experience" and "qualifications" with their female ones. Their behavior is so ingrained, they don't even realize they're doing it.

At the same time, women have internalized this system to the point that they fail to help other females—and sometimes actively work against them.

Tell me if this sounds familiar: a man heads a department. Two women work underneath him, overseeing their respective areas. Both women are more competent than their boss. But instead of working together, crushing their jobs and showing how powerful they can be together, they constantly sabotage each other to win their boss's favor. The man sleeps soundly at night while the women scheme about how to cut each other down and "win."

The same is true in sexual dynamics, at least on the hetero end of the spectrum. Women are ingrained with the idea of "pleasing" and "servicing" men. We compete against each other for male attention. And "The Bachelor" and "The Real Housewives of [fill in the blank]" condition us to throw wine in each other's faces and flip over tables to defeat our female colleagues and friends.

After I talked about this phenomenon with Pam one night, we came up with the title for this chapter. In business, men suck each other off and women cut each other down. We both see it. We're both sick of it. And we both want it to change.

Sexy Business Secret #7

In sex and business, women bear the weight of added expectations while men feel freer to be transactional. Men need to change their double standards. Women need to help each other instead of competing for male approval.

Networking Groups Tell You Everything You Need to Know

I'm part of a female networking group whose membership consists of impressive women from every corner of the business world. From the moment I joined, I was excited by the possibilities. I couldn't wait to get started.

One day, I served on a panel where each woman had to stand up and say who she was, what she did and what she wanted to get from the group. After the other panel members talked about wanting to "connect," "gain leadership skills" and "feel part of a community," I shocked the crowd by saying this:

"My name is Tracy Call. I'm the founder and CEO of Media Bridge. And what I want from you is more business!"

After a few seconds of nervous laughter, the room erupted into a standing ovation. *Wow*, I thought. *I'm not alone! I've just said something every woman in this room has wanted to say for years! Finally, we can act like men and help each other make more money!*

Afterwards, dozens of women ran up to me to tell me how refreshing my business bluntness was. I was *brave*. I had *broken new ground*. I was *so right*.

I went back to my office and waited for the phone to ring with all the new business I was bound to get. Only one woman called, and she never followed through after our initial conversation.

I tell this story because nothing paints a starker contrast between male and female business relationships than the professional networking group. If you think I'm engaging in "bro" stereotyping, I can assure you I'm not. Men in networking groups literally *do* sit around drinking whiskey, smoking cigars and jerking each other off. Okay, they don't *literally* jerk each other off. But they do bend over backward (and sometimes forward) to forge new partnerships, give each other jobs, secure speaking gigs and generally elevate each other's penises. I mean careers.

> "Nothing paints a starker contrast between male and female business relationships than the professional networking group."

In my experience, women in networking groups talk about family. They talk about leadership. They talk about "how to juggle it all." But they rarely take meaningful action to help each other financially. And they almost never directly seek business from each other—even in women's groups where "sharing new business opportunities" is literally in their mission statement.

I don't know about you, but I'd rather act like men in this regard. I'd rather get in a room and talk about all the ways we can make each other more money without worrying about someone thinking we're "too crass," "too direct," "too superficial" or "too aggressive."

Men don't worry about any of that. They see growing their careers, businesses and pocketbooks as their birthright. I don't often advocate for acting like men, but in this case, it's a no-brainer.

Love (& Success) Is Never Having to Say You're Sorry

Man, do women love to apologize. Start counting the times you hear a woman say the words "I'm sorry" in the course of a day, and you'll soon lose track. Turn this into a drinking game, and you'll never be sober again. We apologize in the bedroom. We apologize on the Zoom call. More and more, we even apologize to our kids.

What the hell's going on? What are we so sorry for?

It's simple. As women, we're only successful if we're liked. Call it YSSMS: You Should Smile More Syndrome. We learn the importance of being liked early in our personal relationships, then it bleeds into our work lives as we age.

Men aren't saddled with this baggage. In fact, it's almost the opposite. For them, caring about being liked is a sign of weakness. Depending on your industry, you're more respected for being aggressive, if not ruthless. "Greed is good!" "Coffee is for closers!" But the more "different" you are from a straight white man in business, the more likable you have to be. Being lesbian has always added to the pressure I feel. I can only imagine what it's like to be a Black lesbian, or a Black lesbian with a disability.

This pressure to be liked leads to one thing: perfectionism. Women won't apply for jobs if they don't check every box. Many of us spend all day trying to be liked at work, then come home and try to be liked by our families. It's unachievable and exhausting.

Men have challenges of their own, but they don't have *this* challenge. Most don't think twice about applying for a job they're not qualified for, and most don't care if their kids like them. They also don't think twice when they reward a male employee or hire a friend. But they wonder if a woman is showing "favoritism" by elevating a female employee. *Is Tonya really qualified, or is she just a friend of Stephanie's?*

Since this is a book about sex and business, you might be wondering, "Does this perfectionist double standard translate to the bedroom?" Let me count the ways. Before a woman has sex, she runs through a checklist in her head. *Did I shower? Am I perfectly shaven? Are any of my lady parts jiggling? Should I have eaten that bean burrito for dinner?*

It's simple: in sex and business, women have to be more careful, more self-conscious and more perfect than their male counterparts. Straight men are always ready to go. They don't think about the state of *their* sack before they jump into *yours*. (Okay, that was crass. But you know what? I'm not apologizing.)

The Art of Compartmentalizing

When I played rugby, my women opponents understood the difference between life and competition. We'd crush each other on the pitch, treating each other like mortal enemies for 80 minutes. Then we'd go out after the game and have a beer. That's the only environment where I've seen women compartmentalize their relationships.

On the professional side, some women's groups actually forbid their members from asking for business in certain situations. The rule exists because women don't want to jeopardize their relationships with each other. There's no separating the personal and professional, and perfectionism rears its ugly head once again: *if this business transaction isn't exactly right, then it's going to impact our friendship.* Everything has to be perfectly clean, perfectly friendly, perfectly reciprocal, perfectly perfect.

Guys don't care. Two dudes can get in a fistfight one day and have beers the next, just as women do in rugby. Where women see fear (*this might end our relationship!*), men see opportunity (*whatever, another guy will give me a chance*). The male business attitude smacks of "one-night stand." With women, it's "what if I see Janet tomorrow, and it's really awkward?"

In my perfect world, men would be less transactional in business, and women would be more so. I've carved out a middle ground where I feel like I can be transactional *and* connected in my professional life, and I want more women to feel the same. It's like a marriage. The overall commitment is emotional, but "who's going to take out the garbage?" That's transactional.

We'll only achieve this balance when women stop holding grudges against each other and start raising each other up. Easier said than done. I can be horrible with grudges. When someone pisses me off, I'm done. I cut and run. I'm getting better, but it's still a challenge.

When it comes to raising women up, however, I have zero problems. I love it. I live for it. Most women are hesitant to hire or elevate their fellow females, because if it doesn't work out, then men might see it as "their fault." As my own boss, I don't have to worry about that. I also get to hire all the amazing women who leave their jobs because their male bosses take them for granted.

I enjoy this advantage, but I'd rather it didn't exist.

Afterglow

Fish don't think about how wet they are, and men don't think about how male-centric the business world is. Men constantly use their power to help each other financially. Their female colleagues feel greater and greater pressure to be liked—often resulting in competitive, perfectionist and harmful behavior. In business, as in sex, women have to try harder and do more. Always.

5 Questions

1. Do you feel like you have to be "perfect" in both your personal and professional life?

2. How is that reflected in your bedroom and boardroom behavior?

3. Do you feel like the women in your work environment support each other and lift each other up, or compete against each other and bring each other down?

4. Are you able to separate business and personal transactions, or do you worry about how one might affect the other?

5. Do you find yourself saying "I'm sorry" a lot? If the answer is "yes," did you just feel the need to apologize for that behavior?

PART IV: KEEPING IT HOT

Let's talk about the morning after, and the morning after that. In both business and life, keeping things hot is harder than getting them sizzling in the first place. But it's also essential. In your business and personal lives, boredom and complacency are the kisses of death.

Chapter 8: Sex Starts in the Morning

"It's work having a vagina.
You think it shows up like that to the event?
It doesn't. Every night it's like getting it
ready for its first quinceañera, believe me."

—Amy Schumer

Don Draper: That's how it works. There are no credits on commercials.

Peggy Olson: But you got the Clio.

Don: It's your job. I give you money, you give me ideas.

Peggy: But you never say thank you.

Don: That's what the money's for!

—Mad Men, Season 4

Here's another conversation I once had with a male friend; we'll call this one Pete:

Pete: I have a strong sex drive.

Me: A lot of people do.

Pete: Not my wife. She didn't grow up in that kind of environment.

Me: A sexual one?

Pete: Yeah.

Me: Let me guess, her parents weren't touchy with each other?

Pete: That's an understatement. They didn't even like each other. I told her I'd have sex with her every day if I could. She said, "I have my own career, plus I'm taking care of the kids. And you're gone all the time." I said, "That's why I want to have sex with you. I haven't seen you all day!"

Me: And how did she respond to that?

Pete: She said, "You know, Pete, you can't just come home and expect it right away. Sex starts in the morning."

Me: Pete, I think I'm in love with your wife.

"Sex starts in the morning." I love those five words. They shouldn't be confused with "morning sex," which I need to have more of. They're about the fact that for most people, sexual desire isn't an easy on/off switch.

Most women need priming—some foreplay in the morning so we're thinking about sex all day. Not literal foreplay. Call it "pre-foreplay" or "non-sexual foreplay." A kind gesture. A subtle touch. A suggestive look that plants the sex seeds to grow later.

> "If your libido is insatiable and on a hair trigger, then your professional life is probably on the chaotic side as well."

I know this because I'm one of those women. Some people equate sex with conquest or competition. Some even like angry sex. I couldn't be further away from that. For me, sex comes from connection. If I don't feel a bond with my partner during the day, then it's not easy to jump into having sex at night. If there's an unresolved issue hanging over our heads, then sex is out of the question. I need a hint of intimacy in the morning. A kiss. A cup of coffee handed to me. Something to make me feel loved, or at least seen.

It's the same in business. If you have an insatiable libido that's always on a hair trigger, then your professional life is probably chaotic as well. This is true of many entrepreneurs and visionaries I know, mostly male: they're easily bored. They push others for the sake of pushing them. They exhaust people with their intensity and "work hard, play hard" attitude. Instead of recognizing the million little things their team does right every day, they assume that the occasional raise or party event will keep everyone happy. Then they wonder why their company is a revolving door of talent.

For most women, it's the opposite. You feel like Peggy Olson on "Mad Men." You do all the hard work. The man takes the credit and gets the accolades. The least you deserve is some acknowledgment. A pat on the back. A thank-you.

"Sorry, that's your job," you hear. And that's when you start your own ad agency.

Sexy Business Secret #8

The setup is always as important as the payoff. You can't have one without the other. You can't get to orgasm without feeling a touch of intimacy from the moment you and your partner wake up in the morning. And you can't be satisfied in your job unless you feel like your talents are regularly recognized and your company is investing in your growth.

Catch & Neglect

We all know that person. Maybe we are (or were) that person. It's all about the conquest. Exceeding others' expectations. Landing that lover who everyone thinks is out of their league. Then they do it. They go out, hit it off and actually start dating. But the thrill is soon gone, because if they can land *that* person, then why not go for someone even better?

I call this "Catch & Neglect," and it's as rampant in business as it is in life.

In most one-night stands, the relationship is understood: it's just sex. When it's over, both parties go their separate ways without any further expectations of each other. In Catch & Neglect, one of the parties is purely ego-driven. They love starting relationships. Maintaining them? Not so much.

Catch & Neglect is rampant in virtually all industries, but especially in advertising. Entrepreneurs love nothing more than landing huge clients. It's all about the hunt, adding that Fortune 500 company or sexy startup logo to the website. Once they get them, though—once they wake up next to the client after a few months and smell their metaphorical morning breath—the thrill is gone. Time to fantasize about an even bigger fish.

Problem is, the client isn't stupid. They notice that your "A Team" now has a lot of interns. They notice that it takes hours and days to get answers to their calls, emails and texts instead of seconds and minutes. Eventually, they threaten to leave for another agency that'll give them the attention they deserve. You panic. Spring into action. Take the client out for drinks and dinner. Promise that you'll never take them for granted again.

But it's too late. The trust is gone.

"Sex starts in the morning" is about never taking a great relationship for granted. It's about being consistently proactive. Not waiting for your partner to initiate affection. And not staggering home after cocktails and expecting to have sex on demand (see previous chapter).

> "You can't expect legacy clients to stay with you just because they started with you. And you can't expect top performers to keep working for your company purely out of 'loyalty.'"

It's the same with clients and employees. You can't let great business relationships atrophy. You can't expect legacy clients to stay with you just because they started with you. And you can't expect top performers to keep working for your company purely out of "loyalty."

In advertising, client relationships are often doomed the minute you start hearing things like:

"Your work isn't as creative as it used to be."

"Everyone's talking about our competitor's new campaign, not ours."

"Someone from another agency told us your strategy is wrong. Defend it."

"Why don't you come to us with new ideas anymore?"

"You used to call us back right away. What changed?"

The challenge in keeping any relationship hot is dealing with the blindness of attraction itself. When you feel powerfully drawn to someone, your brain overlooks all the things that will later drive you nuts. With lovers, it's the gum-smacking, the loud gulping, the leaving-the-plates-in-the-sink-instead-of-putting-them-in-the-dishwasher thing.

In business, it might be your prized new employee being late for their first couple of meetings. Or that awesome new client "forgetting" to pay their first bill. And then their second.

In the beginning, you write these behaviors off. *Everything's new. We're just getting started. It's fine.* Sometimes that's true. Other times it's an early warning sign of lack of respect.

Do you need to end relationships at the first sign of trouble? Maybe. Or maybe you just need a little …

Intentional Intensity

In early 2018, I took a sabbatical from work. I called it The Entrepreneurial Stress Test. For one month, I went as far off the grid as you can these days. I set up my employees to handle everything, including answering my emails. I gave my leadership team free range to make decisions. I told everyone that I only wanted to be contacted in an emergency. My actual statement was, "Don't call or text me unless human lives are at stake or the office is burning down." I signed my auto-response emails "Tracy (Don't) Call."

Feeling the burnout after eight years of entrepreneurship, I did something drastic to make clients depend less on me and more on my team. It was a personal "de-stressing" exercise for me. It was a professional stress test for Media Bridge. It ended up being such a life-changing story that *Forbes* wrote an article about it.[3]

I mention this sabbatical because it turned out to be a classic example of "sex starts in the morning." I divided it into two parts. First, Pam and I traveled around Europe with our son, Lincoln. Then she and I went to Paris alone.

During the first part, Pam and I were able to talk without distraction, hold hands and make eye contact. With our then 9-year-old in the room, there was no sex. But we felt more connection in a couple of weeks than we had in years. We banked all that "sex starts in the morning" intimacy for phase two.

Once we got to Paris alone, we committed to each other and to having sex every day. I compare the experience to wearing sunglasses: everything in Paris seemed amber-lit. The Seine. The Eiffel Tower. The people. The brasseries. To this day, every time Pam or I feel frisky from far away, we text each other one word: "Paris?"

Some of you might be thinking, "But isn't 'planned sex' just going through the motions?" I get it. No one wants to put sex on the calendar. But sparks don't always fly for two lovers at the same time. A good sex life has to be intentional and creative. I've made a commitment to initiate intimacy with Pam at least once a week to show her how physically attracted I am to her. She recently sent me a text while she was traveling: "Loved that kiss last night! You haven't kissed me like that in a while!" Trust me, it works.

It's the same in business. When you start a new partnership of any kind, everything is a high. It's new. It's sparkly. The endorphins are pumping. But it isn't sustainable.

---

[3] "Why All Entrepreneurs Should 'Stress Test' How Their Business Performs Without Them," *Forbes*, Barnaby Lashbrooke, 6/25/19.

Eventually you hit a fork in the road: one path says "Platonic," the other "Intentional." You can coast together, take care of each other's basic needs and settle. Or you can get purposeful and set yourself up for a healthy, fun and long-lasting relationship.

In business, that means never taking a client or employee for granted and staying committed to every aspect of their growth. It means being as responsive after two years as you were after two days. Going out for drinks or dinner regularly, not just when there's a problem. Providing employees with not only money and great benefits, but also profit sharing, mental health resources, and serious DEI education and action. It means showing people exactly how they can advance within your organization so they can see a positive future and work toward it.

In short, it means *caring*. And that's fitting. Because at Media Bridge, our mantra is …

"The Best Marketing Strategy Is to Care"

Caring sounds like a touchy-feely topic, but it's way bigger than hugging and holding hands. In business, you can show caring in countless ways, both big and small.

Recently Brian, one of our business development pros, told me that he had changed an in-person meeting with a company to a Zoom meeting to speed things up. "Change it back!" I said. "Tell him we're not in a hurry. We're not a sales organization. We don't have 'hot, warm and cold leads' that we have to 'close.' We start business partnerships based on trust. And we like to meet face to face."

Brian wasn't used to operating that way, but he went with it. He scheduled an in-person meeting for a week later, and it went great. After the company told him they wanted to work with us, he walked up to me and said, "That was huge." The client appreciated our patience and desire to meet in person. We had found their professional G spot.

The business equivalent of "sex in the morning" is Gary Vaynerchuk's saying, "The best marketing strategy: care." You show how much you care when you meet people where they're at, physically and otherwise. My advice to Brian traced back to that fateful 2015 meeting with Mike McGuire. He signaled what kind of a guy he was. I showed up to one of his stores toting a six-pack of beer. We've been colleagues and friends ever since.

Once you establish a truly caring relationship, though, you can't suddenly change it. Whether we realize it or not, we track the nature of our relationships. I put them into two categories: conditional and unconditional.

Conditional relationships are just that: I'll give you one thing if you give me something else in return. These relationships are rooted in practical needs, so they're shallow by nature. And that's fine. I don't need to have a spiritual connection with my mechanic.

Unconditional relationships are the opposite. They're deep. They're personal. They're long term. Simple enough, right? But here's the thing: we don't like it when someone switches our relationship from one category to the other.

My friend Jenny once demanded that I compensate her for insights she'd given me years before during personal conversations. I was shocked that she would turn an unconditional relationship into a conditional one, as if everything that comes out of our mouths—even between friends—carries a price tag. I would never consider asking her to pay me for all the advice and insights I've given her over the years (not to mention the actual money).

Inheritance situations famously move relationships from "unconditional" to "conditional." This nearly happened to me

25 years ago, when two deaths in the family (a grandmother and an aunt, who was also my godmother) resulted in an interesting situation: the two women owned a total of three heirloom diamond rings that needed to be handed down. Conveniently, there were also three granddaughters in the family, including me. Despite the easy math of giving each granddaughter one ring, my two cousins received all three. Was I left out because I was adopted, lesbian, both? I still don't know.

The snub hurt. My dad was furious, and I knew he'd fight for me if I asked him to. But I chose to let it go. Conflict is hard for my dad, and confronting his last remaining sister, who had made the decision on the rings, might have destroyed that important relationship. In the end, unconditional love for my dad defused what could have turned into a highly "conditional" situation all around. It was worth it.

Giftology

People often compare me to Leslie Knope, Amy Poehler's famous character from "Parks and Recreation." I've still never seen the show, but I get the idea: Leslie was the ultimate gift-giver. Her gifts weren't necessarily expensive or elaborate. But they were always thoughtful and meticulously customized to each person.

I'll admit it: I do have a sixth sense for knowing what people like and want. Someone once gave me *Giftology*, a popular book that covers this topic in depth. It's a great book, but as I read it, I didn't think, *Wow, this is groundbreaking!* I thought, *Why didn't I write this first?*

Giftology works because it's the ultimate example of sex starting in the morning. The key is seeing gifts in a broad way. They can be actual gifts. They can come in the form of praise, especially for people who thrive on positive feedback. Or they can be something that you operationalize into your benefits package.

A few small examples:

- When one of our creative directors took a year off to focus on his musical career, I discovered that he once sold his favorite electric guitar because he needed money at the time. I tracked down the guitar and bought it back for him as a going-away present.

- To show support for The Bond Between, one of the Midwest's largest animal rescues and a longtime Media Bridge client, I set up a system where Media Bridge would pay any of our dog-loving employees to fly to Mexico for a brief vacation, as long as they returned with a rescue animal for the nonprofit.

- When we started a media partnership with the Minnesota Twins organization, we took a sizable chunk of our fee money and applied it toward giving employees free tickets to games throughout the season.

- Remember my story from Chapter 3 ("Chemistry"), when I sent a potential client a custom gift of high-end kitchen knives after a less than inspiring initial meeting? That gesture said more than words ever could, cutting through (pardon the pun) to start a meaningful personal and professional relationship.

This gift-centric approach doesn't come naturally to everybody. In fact, I've learned that one of the greatest gifts I can give is coaching other leaders in these areas, even within my own company. Some people are great visionaries or operations geniuses, but they don't realize the impact of simply walking around, saying hello to people and asking them how they're doing.

Hiring the right person and then sitting back and doing nothing is like saying, "I married my soulmate, so I guess we're good for life." If you're in a position of leadership, you need to model kindness and generosity, along with vision and decisiveness.

The Pandemic Test

The March–April 2020 Covid lockdown tested personal and professional relationships like never before. Couples found themselves divided in their emotional responses to the fear and uncertainty, falling on the spectrum from "I don't care, it's not real" to "we're all gonna die!"

Professionally, this period separated the businesses that operate from a "sex starts in the morning" mindset from those that don't. And in times of crisis, you always remember who was there for you and who wasn't.

Frankly, many business leaders freaked out and disappeared in the spring of 2020. That behavior wasn't well received by their employees or their clients. Other leaders hit the panic button and shifted into "scramble for business" mode. That wasn't good, either, as their clients felt their relationships becoming increasingly "conditional."

The companies and leaders who did it right saw the pandemic as a time to strengthen their partnerships. Instead of asking others to help them, they looked for ways to help others.

In that spirit, I need to make a humble brag about Media Bridge. Our team's response to the lockdown was to systematically call our clients and ask them how they were doing. We started conversations: *What can we do to help? How should we change your creative? How should we change your media plan?* We took the midnight texts and phone calls. We said yes to things other agencies said no to. We helped clients change or get out of their media plans if they no longer made sense in the altered media climate.

We did everything from handholding to amateur therapy, and our clients never forgot it. Many of them still walk up to me today and say, "You're the only place that treated us like a true partner during that horrible time. Thank you."

Did we charge for our extra communication and expertise during that time? No, because it fit our core value of "Do the Right Thing." As a result, it just happened to be good for business. Our clients now know without a doubt that we have their backs. They've stayed with us, and they've told their friends about us. Now they're doing the "sex starts in the morning" work *for* us.

Afterglow

The longer you're in any relationship, the more conscientious you need to be. The more often you start each day letting your lover know that you see them, hear them and care about them, the more likely you'll end the day doing the horizontal tango. The more often you show clients and colleagues how much you appreciate them, the more often they'll do the same and deepen your partnership.

5 Questions

1. Do you tend to take others for granted in relationships, or do you feel like others take you for granted?

2. Do you show others the kind of attention and appreciation you expect to receive?

3. Have you ever gotten a great job or promotion because you invested in a relationship early, and that investment eventually paid off?

4. What makes you feel most appreciated in your job?

5. If you could give a meaningful gift to your closest colleague or most beloved client tomorrow, what would it be?

"Just Give Me a Shot!"

When I met Michael, I could tell he wasn't your stereotypical salesman. That's why I hired him.

Media Bridge isn't a "sales organization," and Michael isn't slick or smarmy. He's great at his job because when he meets a potential client, instead of demanding a commitment, he asks for an assignment.

"Just give me a shot," he'll say. "Let me do an audit of your current media campaign. Let me take a peek under the hood of your sales and marketing function. Even if you don't work with us, you'll get valuable expertise that you can use."

Michael's approach works because it's the sales version of "sex starts in the morning." His "give me a shot" is the business version of holding hands. Metaphorically, he doesn't ask to get laid; he engages in foreplay. He gives people a taste of what it's like to work with Media Bridge so they can decide whether or not they want to jump in the professional sack with us.

Michael knows that every new business relationship starts with a dating process. And when he does bring in a new client, he makes sure that they're always appreciated—and never taken for granted.

Chapter 9: Breaking Up Is Hard to Do

Let it go, let it go
Can't hold it back anymore
Let it go, let it go
Turn away and slam the door
I don't care what they're going to say
Let the storm rage on
The cold never bothered me anyway

—"Let It Go," Idina Menzel

The StarHouse retreat center is nestled in a pine forest 7,000 feet above sea level near Boulder, Colorado. I'm here for a leadership retreat, doing an intense breathing exercise with six other entrepreneurs.

Our leader, Finnian Kelly, starts by having us take deep breaths in a slow rhythm. Then he has us pick up the pace. Within minutes, I feel like I'm doing a hard workout.

"Let the energy of your surroundings enter in through the top of your head," Finnian instructs. I do, and an aura forms around me, a bubble incorporating everyone in the room. I feel physically, spiritually and emotionally connected to them.

"Now imagine that you're strapping on a backpack and descending to the bottom of a deep canyon, the Grand Canyon."

I feel myself going deeper and deeper into something thick and dark. It's familiar and unknown at the same time.

"Gather what you feel and put it in your pack," Finnian continues. "Now head back up the hill."

I start to feel very, very heavy.

"Now hold your breath."

Being a competitive person, I decide to push myself hard on this one. I go for one minute. Two minutes. Three minutes. At four minutes, I drift into an alternate space that feels like a natural high—probably what it's like to be on 'shrooms or DMT.

The people around me start to shake, sweat and sob. *What's going on?* I think. Then the wave of emotion breaks over me as well. An energy floods my brain. I've never felt anything like it. I still can't describe it.

My internal backpack flies open. Images of past relationships swirl through my body. Work relationships. Personal relationships. Intimate relationships. Family. Friendship. Love. Sex. Hate. I feel hurt and disappointment, the anger of grudges I've held onto for years.

When I get to the bottom of the pain—when I find the last heavy item in my backpack and hold it up to my face—I see the source of my emotions: *abandonment.*

I can't hold my breath in any longer. I open my mouth and gasp for air.

"Now write in the journal next to you," Finnian tells us. "Write without thinking. Don't stop yourself."

I fling open my journal, grab my pen and write three words: "Let it go." I keep writing them. "Let it go. Let it go. Let it go …"

My hand won't stop.

"Let it go. Let it go. Let it go … "

What am I letting go of?

Sexy Business Secret #9

If you linger in toxic personal relationships, then you probably stay too long in bad jobs too. Maybe even a bad career. Getting out of these relationships is essential. But as we all know, that's easier said than done.

Change Your Narrative

Entrepreneurs are Earth's most pathologically driven people. My clients and colleagues often captained their school teams, and many remain competitive in sports to this day. They run marathons. They play pickleball. Any chance they get, they join a team and play to win.

I'm no exception. I was a high-level athlete in my school years and beyond. Only a badly timed knee injury kept me from competing in the 2010 Vancouver Winter Olympics as a member of the U.S. Women's Bobsled Team. My legs are so strong, they could be insured by Lloyd's of London.

Competitiveness helps you achieve success, but sometimes it comes from a negative place. Many entrepreneurs start their careers with a big chip on their shoulder. They want to make their former boss regret firing them. They want to create a business that outgrows the employer who kept them from reaching their potential. They want to show Mom or Dad that they're worthy of their love.

Unfortunately, negative motivations can only get you so far. If your primary drive centers on "silencing the doubters," "proving everybody wrong," "crushing the competition" or "finally getting the recognition I deserve," then you might succeed in the short term, but you'll eventually hit a ceiling. Chip-on-the-shoulder mindsets in business are like angry sex in the bedroom. They're not about connection. They're about vindication, power and revenge.

The StarHouse breathing exercise showed me that I hold onto negativity and sometimes torture myself with it. I can never unsee that, and my personal development work now focuses on "letting go" in my relationships, starting with my relationship with myself.

Where I used to move through life like a bull in a china shop, I now step calmly and deliberately, like I'm walking through water without making a wake. If a Media Bridge employee chooses to leave us for another job or career, I no longer take it as a personal failure. If their next level of growth requires trying something new, then I let them go and wish them well. In the rare cases when someone tells me that I can't fire toxic Client X because they bring in too much money, I say, "They're not a core value fit." I let it go. I trust that it'll work out for the best. And it always does.

> "I've learned to pick my battles. Or better yet, to stop seeing everything as a battle in the first place."

Letting go isn't about getting soft. I'll always be competitive. I'll never like to lose. And I'll always take a bullet for my family, clients and employees. The difference is that I no longer let my competitive edge stifle my growth. I've learned to pick my battles. Or better yet, to stop seeing everything as a battle in the first place.

When Is It Time?

My friend Tina, who I talked about in the Introduction, felt bored and stuck for so long that she normalized it. Instead of avoiding the negative spaces of stagnancy and frustration, she saw them as her comfort zones.

Maybe your life currently consists of traveling from a toxic boss in the morning to a toxic partner at night. Or maybe you're going through the motions at work with one eye on the clock, then going through the motions in bed with one eye on your phone. Both situations are destructive. The longer you let them go, the harder it is to break free.

Some breakups have come easily for me. When my old boss demanded that I randomly raise a rate on a loyal client, I quit. When "Don't Kiss Me Back" Ian cheated on me with his ex-girlfriend, I ended our relationship. When an employee at a former Media Bridge client made an anti-Semitic crack to one of my Jewish employees, I said "buh-bye" and didn't look back.

But other times, I've held on way too long, as I did with Nick, the credit-repair business guy who's now in jail. The best example happened with the ultimate merger of my personal and professional relationships: I once mixed business with a woman I was dating. When we started, I didn't yet know who I was or what I wanted. As I got to know myself better, I realized that we weren't a good match. We were never on the same page sexually or professionally, and I kept thinking that I could change her by showering her with love and attention.

It wasn't meant to be. We gradually withdrew, and then things got mechanical. Our dual partnerships could have dragged on even longer than they did. But infidelity again reared its ugly head, and I jumped ship.

Bad relationships often trace back to false chemistry and believing that good feelings in the beginning will eventually come back. When they don't, it's easy to enter denial mode.

"Wake up!" your best friend Barb tells you at the party. "Scott's not good for you!"

"You don't know the *real* Scott," you respond. "Only I do. You have no idea what you're talking about!"

Pro tip: Barb is usually right.

Ending a relationship that has passed its sell-by date is hard, but it can also be incredibly fulfilling. Ever left someone you didn't click with sexually for someone you *did* click with? It's transformative. This happens all the time with lesbians who come out later in life. I can't tell you how many times a friend has approached me after sleeping with her first woman and screamed, "Holy shit, I had no idea how great sex could be!"

Coaching People Out

When Jenna told me she was leaving Media Bridge for an entirely different career, I wasn't surprised. She had steadily risen the ranks, but something always seemed to dull her happiness.

Months earlier, I had taken her on a "personal path" journey to discover how she could apply her skills for maximum happiness. I knew that this exercise might ultimately lead her away from me, and it did. In effect, I "coached her out" of her position. Was it hard to let her go? Extremely. But it was the right move for both of us.

Not every breakup has to be painful. Some can be steered into positive territory. Criminal investigators like to say that they'll "follow the evidence wherever it leads." Coaching is the same way. I coach clients, employees and even family members to be happier in their lives, no matter where that takes them. Ninety percent of the time, I end up coaching them "in." The other 10% of the time, I coach them "out": the process leads to a mutual realization that our relationship needs to end, or at least change.

Media Bridge doesn't do traditional employee reviews. Instead, our department leaders conduct quarterly meetings that focus on figuring out what their team members want to do, enjoy doing, are good at doing and have the capacity to do. It's based more on passion than performance. The focus is on helping people grow.

Most Media Bridge employees have been coached in (and up) effectively. A handful have been coached out, and that's to be expected. Sometimes you realize that you aren't a good fit for each other, or that the right seat for a particular person simply doesn't exist.

I've coached out a handful of clients as well. If we discover that a company needs services that we don't offer and never will (e.g., public relations), then we'll refer them to the best agency in that field. If we agree that a client would be better served by creating an internal marketing team instead of continuing to work with us, then we'll help them build that department.

You have to do what's best for everybody, free of agenda. Some people in struggling relationships will engage in couple's therapy—not to solve the root of the issue, but so that a third party will prove them "right." I'm all for bringing in independent experts, but when you do that, you have to accept that they might recommend ending the relationship entirely.

It's never easy when that happens. But if the answer to "what can I do to help you be happy?" is "nothing," then it's time to part ways.

Afterglow

Breaking up is hard to do, but it's also one of the most *empowering* things you can do. In business and life, breaking up is really about letting go. Look at it through that lens, and it will transform from a loss into a gain, and open doors to exciting new places.

5 Questions

1. Have you ever had a "good" breakup in your personal life —one that felt mutual and constructive for both of you?

2. Have you ever been scared to leave a job, then felt surprisingly empowered once you did?

3. Is there some aspect of your relationship with yourself that feels like it needs to change?

4. Do you currently feel energized in your job, or like you're going through the motions?

5. What would you find at the bottom of your personal canyon and put in your metaphorical backpack?

"Will You Take Me Back?"

One of my best friends dated a woman we'll call Sandra. The three of us hung out for years and were a tight-knit group. Until Sandra cheated on my friend.

My feelings on infidelity are no secret at this point, so it should come as no surprise that I immediately cut Sandra out of my life. I couldn't believe what she had done to my friend, and I couldn't forgive her.

Here's where things got complicated: the two women later made amends. Today, my friend is friends with Sandra, and I'm not. I still can't let it go. Sandra's infidelity literally hurt me more than it hurt the woman she cheated on!

I can be the same way in business. Media Bridge has never been fired by a client, but sometimes we've decided to "consciously uncouple" with one. Usually, it's because we were their first media partner, and—like a person wanting to experience other sexual partners after losing their virginity to their first one—they want to sow their wild oats with other agencies.

When the client wants to come back after realizing how good they had it with us, I have to admit: I have a hard time saying yes. *Why couldn't you have seen our value from the beginning?* I think. *Why did you need to leave us in order to appreciate everything we do for you?*

It's not a healthy attitude. I've now taken back one client under the strict guideline that I not work with them directly. And I've also welcomed back a few employees who have seen our value more clearly after leaving us for other jobs. I have more work to do, but I'm learning to let go.

Breaking Up with Yourself

Entrepreneurs are famously possessive about their businesses. "This is my baby! I built it into what it is today!"

I've long felt the same way about Media Bridge. I started it with nothing, took on 100% of the risk and worked my ass off to make it successful. When it comes to sharing the success, I'm totally on board. Profit share. Health benefits. Personal and professional development. I'm all over it. I love it. But when it comes to actual ownership, this baby is mine!

A couple of years ago, something happened that most successful entrepreneurs will experience at some point: my CMO, Toni, told me she wanted to become a partner in the business. Toni was one of my first and best hires. I had watched her blossom into one of the most incredible professionals I've ever seen. Now she wanted to take our relationship to the next level.

Toni had a solid case. She had brought in clients and grown their accounts exponentially. She had earned the trust of everyone around her and added value beyond measure to the business. But I wasn't able to embrace her request until I realized that adding her as a partner wasn't "giving up" part of my business; it was adding to it.

When it comes to ownership, many entrepreneurs need to break up with themselves. Your business will always be your baby. But other people will always help that baby grow and succeed. If they're willing to make a deeper commitment to you, then it might be time to deepen your commitment to them.

Epilogue

Congratulations! We've not only come to the end of this book, we've also come full circle. I just described the moment when I got over my entrepreneurial possessiveness to start a true partnership in business with my CMO, Toni.

My next step in that process was the Love Path in Mexico that my friend Finnian talked about in his foreword to this book. Finnian had long conducted these exercises for romantic couples. I became the first person to request that he do one for a business partnership. The experience was life-changing for both Toni and me, and we've enjoyed a healthy business partnership ever since.

But here's the thing ...

At the time, I thought my decision to approach my business partnership in a similar way to a romantic relationship was innovative.

It was.

I thought it was the ultimate proof of how personal and business relationships run in parallel.

It was.

What I failed to see was the symbolism of doing a non-romantic love path with my business partner before I ever did one with my romantic partner. If someone had tapped me on the shoulder and said, "Hey, Tracy, do you think that might say something about your priorities right now?" I would have denied it. But they would have been right.

About a year later, I was again in Mexico, again with Finnian, again doing a Love Path exercise. But this time, it was with my true love, Pam. It saved our marriage. I realized that I had been so focused on my growing business and building a relationship with Toni that I had lost sight of my relationship with Pam.

Toni and I completed eight months of "counseling" prior to making our partnership legal. We worked extensively with a coach to uncover every personal issue in our backpacks so we could work better as partners. We unearthed issues that neither of us had expressed. It forced us to look each other in the eye and communicate openly about our past experiences and future expectations. What a gift.

Finnian likes to say, "Love isn't enough." In both life and business, you can't just say you'll live "happily ever after" and assume it's going to happen. You have to make it work. You have to address issues as they come up (if not before) and have a plan to handle future conflicts—including how to get "divorced."

I hadn't done that with Pam.

I, the successful entrepreneur and relationship guru, already in the process of writing this book, had allowed a blind spot to emerge in my marriage. I'm happy that I found it in time. Pam and I are now on a similar journey. Our relationship is more open, honest and vulnerable than ever before. And we've never felt closer.

Oh, and remember Tina? I'm happy to say that she's left her career and begun an entirely new one. She's found her sweet spot. Her confidence is off the charts. And she's much happier in her work life. It's just a matter of time before it filters into her personal life as well.

To those who still insist that business and personal relationships are completely different animals, I say, "Is that true in *your* life? Do you really approach *your* professional relationships in the opposite way from your personal ones?"

I'm glad that I rejected the "build a border wall" view years ago. That decision has led to experiences, friendships and growth that I wouldn't trade for anything.

My hope is that you feel more energized now than you did when you started this book. That you've answered the questions I've posed in these pages, learned a few things about yourself, and feel more confident than ever about taking your personal and professional relationships to a more exciting level.

I'm giving you a big Tracy Call hug through the space and time that separate us. Now *we* have a connection and a relationship. And is there anything better than that?

—Tracy

Acknowledgments

*Thank you Marc Conklin for helping me find my voice,
and Antonia Murphy for giving me the confidence to use it.*

About the Author

Tracy Call is an author, a former Team USA bobsled athlete and the founder and CEO of Media Bridge, a Minneapolis-based media and creative agency which has appeared on *Inc's* 5000 Fastest-Growing Private Companies list yearly since 2014. As an activist for social justice, Call led a campaign in Minnesota to defeat a state constitutional amendment that would have made same-sex marriage illegal. She lives in Minneapolis with her partner Pam Kosanke, who is also a former professional athlete and current C-suite-level executive. *G Spot for the C Suite* is Call's first book.

For more information:

Printed in the USA
CPSIA information can be obtained
at www.ICGtesting.com
LVHW071254210923
758824LV00007B/7/J